THE FIRST, THE FASTEST AND THE FAMOUS

A Cavalcade of Croydon Airport Events and Celebrities

Compiled by Douglas Cluett

Design Shirley Edwards

London Borough of Sutton Libraries and Arts Services

Introduction

This book is designed as complementary to the first two books in our *History of Croydon Airport* series: *The First Croydon Airport* and *Croydon Airport: The Great Days*. The response to these books was phenomenal, and our attention was drawn to hitherto unknown sources of both photographs and reminiscences by people the world over.

With very few exceptions, the illustrations featured here were not used in the previous books, although some of the events were mentioned at lesser or greater length. Essentially, *The First, the Fastest and the Famous* is a compilation of photographs of events at Croydon which made news or concerned newsworthy people, in more or less chronological order, but it is not an exhaustive survey of *every* event of note or every famous flier who came to Croydon. Rather, it is an attempt to present a good selection of interesting photographs for the enjoyment of everyone with an interest in the past and, particularly, the history of Croydon Airport.

Thanks are due to many people for their help. First I would like to thank Joanna and Bob for their part in helping to gather some of the pictures used and many pictures not used. From the Library end, there is Val Murphy, whose idea the book was — and who ended up typing it; and of course Roy Smith, Borough Librarian, for deciding to publish it; Mary Batchelor for help in selection and research; and June Broughton for help in very many ways. From the Croydon Airport Society especial thanks are due to E.W.J. (Ted) Crawforth, Mike Marshall, Bert Nash and Tom Samson. Thanks for their help in photography are due to Bert Crawshaw (especially for doing an excellent job for this book in very little time); and to George Jenkinson.

Thanks, too, to all those who supplied or took the pictures in the first place, as acknowledged below, and to many others not mentioned above.

Finally, I would like to express my indebtedness to the late Major Leslie Fitzroy Richard, Chief Aerodrome Officer, Croydon Aerodrome, 1926–1935, who, with splendid foresight, kept a series of scrapbooks covering his years at Croydon. These are now in the Science Museum, and have been an invaluable source of material. Thanks, too, to the Science Museum for making them available, and to John Bagley for his help in this and other respects.

Douglas Cluett
Sutton Central Library
October 1985

Illustrations Acknowledgements

1.	The late Mr. H.P. Jeapes
2,3	Mr. P.T. Capon
4.	Mr. Brian Kempe
5,6	Mr. L.R. Burners via Croydon Airport Society.
7.	The late Charles Lane
8, 9, 10, 11, 13, 15, 16, 18, 19, 23–25, 26–29, 30–32, 33–41, 43, 44, 48, 49, 51, 53–56, 58–61, 64–66, 68–76, 80–83, 87–89, 92–97, 99	Science Museum (Major Richard's scrapbook)
12.	Mr. Bishop
14, 57	Mrs. Pauline Reeves (née Desoutter)
17.	Mr. B. Bacon
20, 22	Bob Learmonth
21, 42, 62	The late A.J. Jackson
45.	Mrs. Julie Little
46, 47	Mrs. Phyllis Lane
52, 77	Mrs. Molly Jones (née Johnson)
62.	Aerodrome Hotel
63.	Photo: E.A. McLennan
67.	Mrs. Peggy Bell (née Salaman) via Croydon Airport Society and Mr. Jack Ful
84.	The late Jack Crowson
85.	Tom Samson (Handford Photography)
90, 91	Capt. Geoffrey Last
98, 104	Flight International
100.	Post Office
101.	Mr. W. A. (Bill) Webb
102, 103	Mr. H.E. (Bert) Nash, via Croydon Airport Society
105.	Mr. Bill Wood, Jnr.
106.	Mr. Ewart Sanders

First published 1985

© Sutton Libraries and Arts Services
Central Library, St. Nicholas Way,
Sutton, Surrey SM1 1EA. Tel. 01-661 5050

ISBN: 0 907335 14 4

Printed and bound in Great Britain by Anchor Brendon Ltd
Tiptree, Essex

1

THE FUTURE GEORGE VI AT CROYDON, 1919

Croydon Airport was formed in 1920 from two earlier flying fields: Beddington Aerodrome, a Royal Flying Corps aerodrome for the defence of London in the First World War; and Waddon Aerodrome, attached to the National Aircraft Factory No. 1 in a field on the eastern side of Plough Lane, Beddington. Beddington Aerodrome was used also for training purposes; and here, in 1919, came Prince Albert, Duke of York, to learn to fly, with No.29 Training Squadron. The photograph shows him at the centre of a group of officers. He succeeded in 'gaining his wings'. Prince Albert later became George VI, in 1936, on the abdication of his brother, Edward VIII (who was also there until his father withdrew his permission to fly).

speed of 123.6 miles per hour, was Captain Franklyn L. Barnard, chief pilot of the Instone Air Line. Barnard's aeroplane was the de Havilland D.H.4a, G-EAMU, *City of York,* Instone Air Line's first aircraft, and one which was in daily service with the airline (picture 2). It had been entered in the race by Sir Samuel Instone, Chairman of Instone's, and picture 3 shows Barnard and Sir Samuel holding the cup between them. The race was, of course, an immense publicity boost for Instone's, who were notable as a very publicity-conscious early airline (later merged into Imperial Airways). Franklyn Barnard also won the King's Cup in July 1925, and was killed test-flying the Bristol Type 99A Badminton for a further attempt on the King's Cup in 1927.

WINNER OF THE FIRST KING'S CUP AIR RACE, MARCH 1922

On the 29th March, 1920, Beddington and Waddon aerodromes were combined to become the customs airport for London — London's chief airport — to be known as the London Terminal Aerodrome, Croydon. One of the two airlines to use Croydon from the start was the Instone Air Line. An important factor in the development of the infant aircraft industry was aerial racing, and this was also a feature of life at Croydon in the early '20s. From its start, the King's Cup Air Race was the most important and most news-worthy air-racing event in Britain. Its name derived from a cup presented by George V, and the race was open to all British aircraft, competing on a handicap basis. The first-ever King's Cup started at 9am from Croydon on 8th September 1922 and involved two days' cross-country flying. Twenty-one aircraft started, and the first day's route was to Glasgow via Birmingham and Newcastle. After an over-night stop, the second day saw a return to Croydon via Manchester and Bristol. There was bad weather on both days, with high-gusting winds. Eleven contestants completed the 810 mile course. The winner, with a flying time of 6 hours, 32 minutes and 50 seconds, at an average

AMERICAN ROUND-THE-WORLD FLIGHT AT CROYDON, MARCH 1924

The first circumnavigation of the world by aeroplane was completed, in stages, by two Douglas World Cruisers, built for the purpose, in 1924. Four machines left the Douglas Aircraft Company's factory at Santa Monica, California, on March 17th. The flight was sponsored by the U.S. Army Air Service and the U.S. Navy. The single-engined biplanes (with 400 hp Liberty engines) were named *Boston, Chicago, New Orleans,* and *Seattle.* Each aircraft had a crew of two. On April 6th, equipped with floats, they took off from Lake Washington, near Seattle, flew to Japan via Canada, Alaska, and the Aleutians, reaching Tokyo on May 24th — or three of them did, *Seattle* having crashed in Alaska. (The crew made their way to safety after being missing for ten days.) At Calcutta, reached on the 1st of July, floats were exchanged for wheels and they flew on over India and Asia Minor to Europe (continued over).

DWC No.3: *Boston,* being taken over the aircraft level-crossing across Plough Lane. A hangar is to the right, but on the left the house is part of the buildings of New Barn Farm, still operating on the airport site at this time.
5. *Right:* Lt. Leigh Wade, pilot of *Boston* with an unidentified man at Croydon.

5

4

On July 16th the three aircraft reached Croydon from Paris, and left on the following day for the Blackburn Aeroplane Company's works at Brough in Yorkshire to be overhauled and re-fitted with floats for the return to America over the Atlantic via the Orkneys, Iceland, and Greenland. On the way to Iceland, *Boston* was lost when it force-landed on the sea, and was wrecked during a salvage attempt by the USS *Richmond*. On the 31st August, *Chicago* and *New Orleans*, having been re-engined in Greenland, reached Labrador. At Nova Scotia they were joined by the prototype DWC, now named *Boston II*, manned by Wade and Ogden, the crew of the lost *Boston. Chicago* and *New Orleans*, crewed by Lts. Lowell Smith and Leslie Arnold, and Lts. Erik Nelson and John Harding respectively, had flown 26,345 miles (or 27,553, according to another source) in a flying time of 15 days, 3 hours, and 7 minutes.

6. *Left to right:* DWCs Nos. 2: *Chicago;* 3: *Boston;* 4: *New Orleans,* lined up at Croydon.

7   ALAN COBHAM'S RETURN FROM THE CAPE, MARCH 1926

Cobham was, in 1925, perhaps the most famous British airman, and the aircraft, a D.H.50J, G-EBFO, in which he flew to Cape Town and back in five months in 1925/6, became probably the most famous contemporary British aeroplane. Cobham, working for de Havilland, had flown the prototype D.H.50, G-EBFN, to victory in the International Air Traffic Competition in 1923, gaining first prize with 999 points out of 1,000; and winning the King's Cup Race with it in 1924. 'FO was the second D.H.50, and in this Cobham made the long-distance flights that earned him his knighthood. The first was in 1924, flying Sir Sefton Brancker, Director of Civil Aviation, on a survey flight to India and Burma. Then, on 16th November, 1925, Cobham took off from Croydon in G-EBFO (now modified to a D.H.50J by the substitution of a more powerful engine) with A.B. Elliott (engineer) and B.W.G. Emmott, a Gaumont ciné-photographer. With excellent organisation, the 8,000 miles to the Cape were flown to reach Cape Town on 17th February 1926. After an even more speedy return trip, Cobham touched down at Croydon at 4.20pm on 13th March, 1926. This was the second successful flight from England to the Cape, but the first to be made in a single aircraft throughout. It was the first return flight from England to South Africa; and it was accomplished in 15 days' flying. In this photograph, Cobham is in the middle at the front, with a helmeted policeman behind his right shoulder. His aircraft is on the right behind the crowd, just past the port wing-tip of the big Handley Page W8, G-EBBI, *Prince Henry*. Alan Cobham was knighted later in 1926 after another pioneering flight, to Australia, in G-EBFO.

8

PASSENGERS AND PILOT ON THE FIRST FLIGHT OF THE FIRST EMPIRE AIR ROUTE, DECEMBER 1926

Just after dawn on Saturday 18th December, 1926, 'the first air liner to India' (for the time being it was going as far as Cairo only) left Croydon Airport. It was a de Havilland D.H.66 Hercules, a new fourteen-seater, triple-engined aircraft designed for the Cairo-Karachi air route. Three had been built and delivered to Imperial Airways, since 1924 the government's 'chosen instrument' for civil airline operation, with its fleet based at Croydon. The Hercules to inaugurate the first leg of the new route was G-EBMY, later to be named *City of Baghdad*. It was the third to be built. It and its sister were to be spaced out along the route, and would operate a regular fortnightly service from January 7th. Pictured here, about to leave on G-EBMY, are (*left to right*): Air Commodore A.G. Weir, Mrs J.G. Weir, Capt. T.A. Gladstone (organiser of the Cairo-Kisumu air route), Air Vice Marshal Sir William Sefton Brancker (Director of Civil Aviation) who had surveyed the route with Cobham, and the pilot, C.F. Wolley Dod. The service was hailed as one which would bring India 'a week nearer London' (the total time to Delhi was about twelve days).

LINDBERGH FLIES IN, MAY 1927

The arrival at Croydon Airport of Charles Lindbergh, on Sunday the 29th of May, 1927, brought more people to the airport than on any other day in its history; indeed they were the largest crowd to assemble at any airport until the return of the Beatles from the USA, to Heathrow, in 1963 at the height of 'Beatlemania'. Lindbergh arrived at Croydon in the afternoon, eight days after he had touched-down in Paris after thirty-three hours in the air at the end of the first successful solo Atlantic crossing, a distance of 3,610 miles. He had come on to Croydon via Brussels, but the welcome at Croydon far exceeded anything seen there or at his first landing, the publicity machine having had time to roll and generate almost mass-hysteria. Lindbergh's aircraft, a Ryan NYP single-engined high-wing monoplane, *Spirit of St. Louis,* was accompanied from over the Thames by a host of other aircraft carrying newspaper reporters and photographers, jostling for position.

9: The Ryan NYP approaching Croydon followd by (*left to right*): a de Havilland D.H.50 piloted by Captain R.H. McIntosh ('All Weather Mac') — commissioned by *The Daily Sketch;* a Handley Page W 10, G-EBMR, *City of Pretoria;* and a Handley Page W 9, G-EBLE, *City of New York* piloted by Colonel F.F. Minchin. 10: Lindbergh standing by a car, presumably hired, at Croydon. 11: A group of Croydon people having themselves photographed beside Lindbergh's car, with the camera in exactly the same position. These two pictures are from the scrapbook of Major Richard, aerodrome controller, who is second from the left in this picture. On the left, is 'Robinson' — presumably Captain 'Scruffy' Robinson of Imperial Airways. The third figure from the left is labelled 'Plaister'. 12: (OVER): Lindbergh, with no help from the crowd, landing at Croydon.

12: When Lindbergh came in to land the crowd broke all restraint and surged across the airfield, barely letting Lindbergh down at all, and preventing any chance of his escort landing after him. About thirty aircraft were left aloft, with their pilots anxiously watching their fuel gauges. One aircraft with an experienced Croydon pilot got down, and one landed in a South Croydon field out of petrol. The rest dispersed to other aerodromes. There was fear that *Spirit of St. Louis* would be torn to shreds by souvenir hunters, and she was taken over to the newly-completed and empty hangars by Purley Way, part of the rebuilding and re-arranging of the airport then in progress; probably the first aircraft to be sheltered there. Charles Grey, editor of *The Aeroplane* castigated both the control arrangements and the behaviour of the crowd on that day. The crowd, he wrote, "behaved just like a lot of foreigners . . ."

MISS COLUMBIA AT CROYDON AFTER TRANSATLANTIC FLIGHT (CHAMBERLIN AND LEVINE), JULY 1927

Saturday, July 2nd, 1927, saw the first visit to Croydon of the transatlantic aircraft *Miss Columbia* and of the eccentric millionaire, Charles Levine, president of the Columbia Aircraft Corporation. Both recur, weaving in and out of the story of inter-war Croydon Airport. *Miss Columbia* was a Bellanca W.B.2, and she had just flown from New York to Berlin, piloted by Clarence Chamberlin. Levine, the owner, was the first transatlantic passenger by aeroplane. It was the latter's temperament that lost Chamberlin the chance of flying to Europe before Lindbergh, because he fell out with Bert Acosta, intended second pilot on the trip — and then with a substitute — and so delayed the start. In the end, just Levine (a non-flyer) accompanied Chamberlin. Perhaps this is what he had always intended, but his delays and Lindbergh's success meant he had lost the chance of winning the Raymond Orteig award of $25,000 offered for the first non-stop aeroplane flight between New York and Paris. *Miss Columbia*'s flight began on June 4th, 1927, and Chamberlin announced the intention of beating Lindbergh's record. The first landing was about 100 miles short of Berlin, with empty tanks. After one more forced landing they reached Tempelhof on June 7th. The non-stop part of their flight exceeded Lindbergh's by 300 miles but took nine hours longer, and Lindbergh had grabbed all the publicity. *The Aeroplane* of July 7th said of their subsequent arrival at Croydon: "... There was a large crowd of police present to greet them [picture 13], but the number of spectators present about equalled the number of police present when Capt. Lindbergh arrived on that famous Sunday afternoon in the brave days of old ..."

13 AN OFFICIAL RECEPTION. Mr. Chamberlin and Mr. Levine, in the Bellanca monoplane (Wright Whirlwind) arriving at Croydon. They were received by the Home Secretary's Force in force.

14: *Miss Columbia* at Croydon. The figure on the far left is the Croydon-based aircraft maufacturer, Marcel Desoutter, by whose hangar the aircraft is parked. *Miss Columbia* returned to Paris, where Levine quarrelled with Chamberlin, and then with a French replacement pilot. He then (despite having no pilot's licence) flew *Miss Columbia* solo back to Croydon and landed her with great difficulty, and much danger to himself and everybody else.

14

10

FIRST APPEARANCE OF THE ROHRBACH ROLAND AT CROYDON, SUMMER 1927

The Rohrbach Ro VIII Roland I, the first transport aircraft to be produced by the Rohrbach-Metall-Flugzeugbau GmbH, was test-flown in 1926. It was a triple-engined high-wing monoplane. Dr. Ing Rohrbach had worked for the Zeppelin-Werke GmbH and had founded his own firm in 1922.

The prototype, D-991, later named *Zugspitze* (a mountain in West Germany), was delivered to Deutsche Luft Hansa (predecessor of Lufthansa) in 1926. It was followed by five more in 1927, in which year DLH began operating them on the Berlin-London route. The Roland I seated ten passengers in its cabin; but for the crew there was an open two-seater cockpit just forward of the leading edge of the wing.

D-991 is shown here on its first visit to Croydon in late July or early August, 1927.

16

15

11

17

FIRST FLIGHT AT THE AGE OF 92 (ALMOST), AUGUST 1927

On Tuesday the 16th of August, 1927, Mrs Elizabeth Reeves, aged almost 92, the oldest inhabitant of Tate's Almshouses, Mitcham, made her first flight in an aeroplane, accompanied by her grandson, Frederick Priestly, an ex-RAF man; and a Mr. W. Field. Mrs Reeves, who wore "a black plush coat with beaver trimming; black poke bonnet and carried a dolman [a loose jacket] of the Victorian period" (*Evening Standard*), was travelling to Cologne to celebrate her 92nd birthday on the coming Friday, on which day she flew back to Croydon. Mrs Reeves was reportedly delighted by the experience: "I really don't feel at all afraid, but I had two small nips of whisky before I left home", she was quoted in the *Daily Mail* as saying. Her pilot was a 'Mr. S. Wheeler', and this was probably Samuel J. Wheeler, Imperial Airways pilot; and her aircraft will presumably have been an Armstrong Whitworth Argosy. Not only had Mrs Reeves not flown before, but this was her first trip abroad. "I don't consider myself old", Mrs Reeves told the *Daily Mirror*; and the *Standard* quoted her as saying: "I hope to celebrate my 100th birthday by another long flight, perhaps across the Atlantic". Unfortunately, however, she died two years later.

WORLD FLIERS DUE AT CROYDON TO-DAY.

ATLANTIC DASH IN YELLOW AIRPLANE.

A BRILLIANT yellow airplane, the name Pride of Detroit painted in black letters on the fuselage, left Harbour Grace, Newfoundland, yesterday morning for London on the first stage of a round-the-world flight.

The pilots are two Americans, William Brock and Edward Schlee; and it is expected that the airplane will reach Croydon this morning.

Weather reports from the Atlantic were excellent at the start of the flight, although the airmen were met by a head wind.

'Seaton, Devon'. This still did not pinpoint their position for them, because their maps were too small-scale to include Seaton; but at least they knew they were over England, and roughly which direction to fly for London and Croydon. They found their way to Croydon by 10.33am, earlier than most people expected, and only about fifty people were there to welcome them: partly because of the time, and confusion about whether or not they were going straight to the Continent; and partly because, as with *Miss Columbia*, Lindbergh seemed just about to have drained the pool of hero-worship for transatlantic fliers. They had used only two gallons of oil from Newfoundland, and — "British engine-designers please note", said Charles Grey in *The Aeroplane* — only about half their load of petrol.

18: Headlines from a contemporary newspaper.   19: *Pride of Detroit* at Croydon, 28th August. The two legs, one arm, and half a back on the extreme right of the picture belong to Major Leslie Richard, airport controller.

FIRST TRANSATLANTIC FLIGHT TO MAKE FIRST TOUCHDOWN AT CROYDON, AUGUST 1927

In the wake of Lindbergh, and Chamberlin and Levine, came William S. Brock and Edward F. Schlee, in a Stinson Detroiter named *Pride of Detroit*. Schlee and Brock were flying the Atlantic as the first leg of an attempt to fly round the world in fifteen days. They got as far as Tokyo, but, on pleas from home, abandoned a projected 4,520-mile Pacific crossing. Like *Spirit of St. Louis* and *Miss Columbia, Pride of Detroit* was powered by a single Wright Whirlwind engine, and was a high-wing monoplane.

Brock and Schlee left Newfoundland at 11.14am on Saturday 27th August, 1927. After encountering strong headwinds over the ocean, and flying the last four hundred miles more or less blind, in cloud and mist, they made landfall over Devon or Cornwall, but could not identify their position, even when they were sighted over Plymouth at about 7am on Sunday.

Reaching Seaton, they dropped messages and someone scratched in chalk on an asphalt road:

19

BILL LANCASTER AND CHUBBIE MILLER LEAVE ON FIRST ATTEMPT TO FLY TO AUSTRALIA, OCTOBER 1927

When ex-Flying Officer Bill Lancaster and Mrs. 'Chubbie' Miller left Croydon on 14th October, 1927, in an attempt to make the first flight from Britan to Australia, they also began a romantic, dramatic and tragic personal story, which ended in Lancaster's death by thirst in the Sahara desert, six years later. Lancaster met Chubbie Miller when he was planning his trip. She was an Australian, married, not very successfully, to an Australian journalist whom she had left behind on a six-month trip to Britain. Chubbie decided she must fly home with Lancaster and offered to help finance the trip through American contacts. Lancaster, too, was married, and it was to be purely a business arrangement. Lancaster's aircraft was an Avro Avian, G-EBTU, *Red Rose* (of Lancaster!) and it had A.D.C. Cirrus II engines, built at Croydon. Lancaster's parents, wife, and two daughters, watched the take-off, and the wife of the Australian High Commissioner made a speech. It look Lancaster and Miller five months to reach Australia, with one major and several minor mishaps on the way. They were not the first to get there by air: Bert Hinkler, starting months afterwards, beat them to it, but Chubbie was the first women to fly (albeit as a passenger) to Australia. By the time they got there they had become lovers. Neither returned home, but went to live together in America. Later, Chubbie, in Bill's absence, found a new lover, who was shot dead on Lancaster's return, and Bill stood trial for murder, but was acquitted. Their joint story ended when, with both of them back in England, Lancaster set out to recoup his fortunes by beating Amy Johnson's record to South Africa. He set out in April 1933 in a late mark of Avian. His route took him across the Sahara, over which he disappeared. Twenty-nine years later the wreck of his aircraft was found with his partially-mummified body still in it, and a diary which he had kept for eight days whilst he died of thirst. On the seventh day he wrote for the woman he still loved: "Chubbie, *give up flying* [she had herself become a pilot] (you won't make any money at it now)." There were two photographs of Chubbie in his wallet.

20: Bill and Chubbie before take-off on October 14th, 1927. 21: Bill Lancaster beside *Red Rose*. 22: The seventh day of Bill's last days in the desert, as written in his log book.

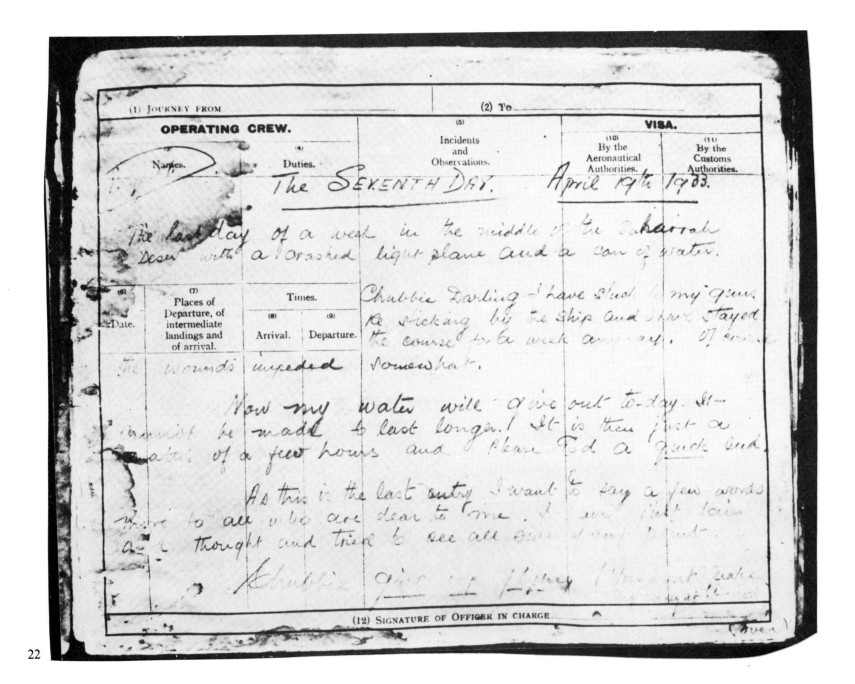

VISIT OF THE KING OF AFGHANISTAN, MARCH 1928

On Wednesday March 21st, 1928, His Majesty King Amanullah of Afghanistan paid an official visit to Croydon Airport. The rebuilt or 'second Croydon Airport' was now in existence, and in use, along the newly-built Purley Way, but not yet officially opened. The King was received by Sir Samuel Hoare, Secretary of State for Air, and Sir Sefton Brancker, Director of Civil Aviation; and he and his retinue were taken for a tour of the new buildings and aerodrome where the usual preponderance of foreign aircraft over British to be seen was balanced on this occasion by specially brought-in club and private light aircraft. The King, with Sir Samuel and Sir Sefton, was taken on a twenty-five minutes' flight over London in an Imperial Airways Argosy.

King Amanullah, in 1928, had only another year to reign. He had come to the throne in 1919, on the assassination of his father, and immediately started a war with British India. Defeated, he nevertheless negotiated the independence of Afghanistan as a sovereign state. His attempts to modernise his country too quickly, and especially to emancipate women, were the cause of a revolution in 1929, in which he was deposed, living in exile in Rome until his death in 1960 (he had, in 1941, tried to enlist German aid to regain his throne).

23: His Majesty disembarks from the Argosy. The bowler-hatted man with the cane was named Robertson, possibly Charles P. Robertson, Head of Press Section, Air Ministry. 24: "King Amanullah appeared to be specially interested in the presence of two lady pilots", said a newspaper account, "— Miss Spooner of the London Club and Miss Brown of the Lancashire Club". This is not Winifred Spooner, and must be Winifred Sawley Brown, who got her

23

pilot's licence in 1927 and won the King's Cup Air Race in 1930, flying the Avro Avian G-EBVZ, presumably the aircraft by which she is standing (she acquired it in January 1928). In Major Richard's scrapbook, this photograph is labelled: "Inspecting Pilot of Avian"; and a later picture: "Woman pilot further inspected"!

24

16

25

25: His Majesty is led across the roof to the control tower. This is a very good and very unusual view of this walkway and the roof of the new main administrative building. The dome of the booking and concourse hall is behind.

LADY MAUDE HOARE OFFICIALLY OPENS THE NEW AIRPORT, MAY 1928

Although the airport administration had been moved to the new buildings in January, it was not until the 2nd of May that the official opening ceremony was performed by Lady Maude Hoare, wife of Sir Samuel, who unveiled a bronze plaque, now lost from the building (see *The First Croydon Airport*, p.79), unlocked the door, declared the terminal building open, and made a short speech; all this in the presence of "a very representative gathering of officials of the Air Ministry, of both British and foreign aircraft operating firms and of the British Aircraft Industry" (*The Aeroplane*). The buildings were of concrete blocks, with a steel frame. This was now the most modern and best-equipped airport in Europe, and for some years set the standard for others. Today the terminal building is listed as of architectural and historic interest, and it is hoped that, through the Croydon Airport Society, founded in 1978, a museum will be established in the building in the next two or three years by courtesy of its present owners, Guardian Royal Exchange Assurance plc.

26: In front of the main doors of the terminal building (*left to right*) are: Sir Samuel Hoare, Secretary of State for Air; Lady Maude; Sir Sefton Brancker, Director of Civil Aviation; the Deputy Director of Civil Aviation; Major Richard, Civil Aviation Traffic Officer (i.e. airport controller); Major Lovatt, representative of the

26

building contractors, Wilson Lovatt and Son Ltd. of Wolverhampton. (The design was a product of the Building and Works Department of the Air Ministry, with no known single architect.)

27: The scene in front of the building. The semi-circular porch canopy has now gone, but it is hoped that this will be replaced soon. On the right is the Aerodrome Hotel, still functioning today with its original name, built as part of the contract and as part of the aerodrome.

27

FIRST EAST-TO-WEST TRANSATLANTIC FLIERS AT CROYDON, JULY 1928

The first successful east-to-west Atlantic crossing in an aeroplane was made by two Germans and an Irishman, between April 12th and 13th, 1928; and on Monday July 2nd they arrived at Croydon with their Junkers W-33L, *Bremen,* on their way to Ireland, and were entertained to lunch at the Savoy by the Royal Aeronautical Club, the Royal Aeronautical Society, the Air League, and the Society of British Aircraft Constructors. Captain Hermann Köhl and Baron Gunther von Hünefeld had been among a group making the first attempt to gain transatlantic honours for Germany in 1927, with two aircraft, *Bremen* and *Europa.* On that occasion *Bremen* got further but was forced back by bad weather. In 1928 Köhl and von Hünefeld decided to try again, this time starting from Ireland instead of Germany. Köhl had been dismissed from Deutsche Luft Hansa for taking part in such a foolhardy venture. He was to be pilot, and von Hünefeld would finance the trip. In Ireland they made the acquaintance of Commandant James C. Fitzmaurice of the Irish Free State Army Corps, who persuaded them to let him take part in the flight. He had once before tried to cross the Atlantic, with Captain Robert McIntosh, but they too were forced back by bad weather. They left Baldonnel aerodrome, near Dublin, on Thursday April 12th at 5am. Köhl and Fitzmaurice shared the flying,

(*over*)

29

and von Hünefeld navigated. Progress during the day was good, but after dark they met dense fog, and then head-winds so strong that they could average only 56 mph against them. They reached Labrador in a snow blizzard (they had been flying along the entire coast of Newfoundland without knowing it) and Köhl, worried about fuel, made a landing on what looked like the first suitable place, Greenby Island, but in doing so damaged the undercarriage and airscrew through his tiredness and the hostile terrain. They were succoured by the fourteen people who lived on the island, and rescued by air; though one of their rescuers, Floyd Bennett, who had flown Byrd over the North Pole in 1926, was taken ill on the way and died of pneumonia; which cast a shadow over their triumph in flying non-stop to America from Europe, in 36 and a half hours, in appalling conditions. Remembering these conditions over the Atlantic, it was perhaps not inappropriate that, on July 2nd, according to *The Aeroplane*: ". . . owing to a head wind they did not arrive at Croydon till 14.15 hours, so the lunch was somewhat delayed".

30

28 (*page 19*): The Junkers W-33L *Bremen* comes in over 'C' hangar block, Croydon. 29: A bouquet of flowers is presented to Captain Köhl at Croydon in front of *Bremen*. 30: Left to right in front row: (Col. Edwards); Baron von Hünefeld; Colonel Fitzmaurice; Commander Harold Perrin, Secretary of the Royal Aero Club; Captain Köhl.

LEVINE AGAIN, AUGUST 1928

In August 1928 the eccentric millionaire Charles Levine was again at Croydon preparing for an attempt at an east to west Atlantic flight. The aircraft intended to make the crossing was a Junkers W.33, similar to Köhl and von Hünefeld's *Bremen* (picture 31). The pilot was to be Bert Acosta (despite Levine having quarrelled with him during the preliminaries to the *Miss Columbia* trip — see p. 10). Also involved was a Miss Mabel Boll (known as 'Mibs') described as an American socialite, who wanted to be flown across the Atlantic and was offering $25,000 to anyone who would do so.

The Aeroplane on August 22nd, 1928, said: "Miss Boll, Mr. Bert Acosta and Mr. Levine propose to start from Croydon for New York as soon as weather conditions are favourable . . . and a runway has been marked out from the Control Tower straight across the old Plough Lane level crossing. The pilot believes he will be in the air before he reaches the level crossing, and we hope this will be the case, not only for the sake of those in the aeroplane but also on account of those householders in Wallington who live in the direct line of flight, and who will probably be topping their breakfast egg about the time of the take-off."

By September 3rd *The Times* was reporting that Mr. Levine had booked a ticket back to New York on the liner *Leviathan*, and would, if the weather was not immediately favourable, entrust the flight to Mr. Acosta with Miss Boll as passenger. By September 6th, Levine had left Cherbourg in the *Leviathan*, having flown there from Paris and had his aircraft seized on landing because Bert Acosta, as pilot, did not have a log book, and the papers of the 'four passengers' were not in order. Levine was allowed to leave but his friends were detained to be charged with failing to comply with police regulations. On September 14th *The Times* reported that Mabel Boll had also left Cherbourg by boat for the States, and that the Junkers had been seized by the Customs authorities, as Customs and flying dues had not been paid. Miss Boll never did get her Atlantic flight.

Picture 32 shows Levine (left), Mibs Boll, and Bert Acosta, in front of the Junkers W.33 at Croydon.

33

RECORD FLIGHT TO BERLIN WITH FIRST ADC CIRRUS HERMES ENGINE, OCTOBER 1928

The Aircraft Disposal Company, which occupied the former National Aircraft Factory No. 1 buildings at Croydon, had been formed to dispose of surplus World War I military aircraft and spares, but by 1928 was chiefly manufacturing aircraft engines. On the 19th of October, 1928, Neville Stack, their chief pilot, flew to Berlin (620 miles) in record time in an Avro Avian IV, G-AAAT, powered by the first production 105 hp ADC Cirrus Hermes I engine. At least two current printed sources give the elapsed time as 4 hours, 52 minutes non-stop, although *The Aeroplane* of October 24th, 1928, in its 'Croydon Notes' said that he left at 10.53 hours and arrived in Berlin at 15.55 hours; though adding: "Whether the latter is G.M.T. or Central European Time, one hour later, and whether the time taken was just over four or just over five hours cannot at the moment be discovered. But in any case the flight, aided by a strong following wind, is among the fastest to Berlin yet made." (This would have made his time either 5 hours 2 mins or 6 hours 2 mins). Beyond Captain Stack, and his Avian (with the engine running) in the photograph, are the ADC hangars (Croydon hangar block 'C').

34   35

34: FILM STARS MEET LADY MOUNTBATTEN ON AN IMPERIAL AIRWAYS ARGOSY, 1929

This picture appeared in *AIRWAYS* magazine in December 1929 and shows husband-and-wife film stars, Douglas Fairbanks (left) and Mary Pickford (at top of steps), with Edwina, Lady Mountbatten (shaking hands with Douglas Fairbanks). Mary Pickford's brother, Jack, is between her and Douglas Fairbanks. They were all about to fly from Croydon to Paris in an Armstrong Whitworth Argosy.

35: LADY BAILEY BACK AT CROYDON AT END OF TEN MONTHS' TRIP TO THE CAPE, JANUARY 1929

On a cold January day (Wednesday the 16th) in 1929, Mary (Lady) Bailey arrived back at Croydon after having flown 18,000 miles in ten months to Cape Town and back. She had a very casual approach to flying, and said she had just gone to see her husband (the South African millionaire Sir Abe Bailey), and, "after finding the outward journey not too difficult, thought it would be interesting to fly back" (Wendy Brown: *The sky's the limit*, 1979). In fact, the trip had not been without incident, she having crashed the D.H.60 Moth, G-EBSF, in which she left Croydon on March 9th, 1928, on the way out, and the replacement Moth, G-EBTG (to which G-EBSF's Croydon-built ADC Cirrus II engine had been transferred), on the way back, causing a four-months' delay for repairs. Lady Bailey, daughter of the Irish peer Lord Rossmore of Monaghan, had married Bailey in 1911, and already had five children when she took up flying, qualifying as a pilot in 1926. Her Cape flight made her the first woman to fly solo to South Africa, and the route back which she chose had never been flown before by anybody. She also, in 1927, had set a new altitude record of 17,283 feet (in a Gipsy Moth with Mrs Geoffrey de Havilland as passenger). The photograph shows her back at Croydon, with two of her daughters.

"On the "tar-mac" at Croydon.
Regards to Major Richard

Clarence de Young
D.C.A. - U.S.A.

36

24

CLARENCE YOUNG, CHIEF OF CIVIL AVIATION IN THE U.S., FLIES OWN AIRCRAFT INTO CROYDON, APRIL 1929

In 1929, Major Clarence M. Young, Chief of the Bureau of Aeronautics of the United States Department of Commerce — the 'Director of Civil Aviation' of the United States, undertook a 2,000 mile official tour of Europe, flying himself, in a Stearman biplane with a Wright Whirlwind engine. He spent some six weeks visiting France, Italy, Germany, Belgium and Great Britain to study air transport conditions in those countries. In April he was at Croydon.

In an interview published in *Flight* in April, 1929, Major Young was asked: "How do the English airliners and aerodromes compare with those of the United States?" "Croydon is a very good aerodrome", he replied, "and the things that impressed me most about it were the administration buildings and facilities for controlling the aerodrome and the excellent accommodation afforded to passengers as well as to shippers and importers of merchandise. As to the question of the airline itself [presumably Imperial Airways], the impressive thing is the constant communication which the aerodrome has with the various aircraft *en route.*" "So you would class Croydon as a first-class station?" "Yes, I would surely call it an aerodrome of the first class, particularly in view of the improvements which are being made there, like the increase of the landing area. The building and equipment at Croydon I consider to be of outstanding merit."

36: Major Young's Stearman in front of the control tower at Croydon. 37: Major Young by his aircraft. Both pictures are inscribed to Major Richard, airport controller, and come from his scrapbook.

37

38

CHARLES KINGSFORD-SMITH AND *SOUTHERN CROSS*, JULY 1929

Australia's most famous aviator, and one of the world's greatest, first flew into Croydon Airport on July 10th, 1929. He had flown from Australia, with his co-pilot, Charles Ulm; his navigator, H.A. Litchfield; and his radio-operator, T.H. McWilliams, in a record time which varies from one printed source to another, but appears to have been twelve days and either fourteen hours eighteen minutes, or twenty-one hours eighteen minutes. The first leg of their flight across Australia, starting on the 31st March, ended when they were forced down by running out of fuel as a result of getting lost in bad visibility, and were missing for twelve days in the bush. They were rescued, however, and left Wyndham, in Western Australia, on June 25th. Whilst in England, Kingsford-Smith and Ulm wished to negotiate the purchase of aircraft for their newly-founded Australian National Airways. The aircraft in which they reached Croydon was a non-standard Fokker F.VII-3m which had been specially built for an arctic expedition in 1926. It had extra-large wings, 220 hp Wright Whirlwind engines, and a modified rudder. It was named *Southern Cross*. When 'Smithy' and his crew returned to Australia by boat, *Southern Cross* was overhauled in Holland by the Fokker company and Smith later returned (in 1930) to collect her, coming again to Croydon before flying from Ireland to Newfoundland in 31 hours, after which *Southern Cross* was shipped home to Australia.

38: *Southern Cross* at Croydon, 10th July, 1929.   39: Kingsford-Smith and his crew leave *Southern Cross*; 'Smithy' is second from right, with cigarette; Charles Ulm is second from left.

39

Here are two pictures of the event from Major Richard's scrapbook: 40: The lady on the left is Mrs. M.E. Dickin, who founded the PDSA in 1917; next to her is Sir Sefton Brancker; and the tall figure between them is Major Leslie Richard. April Day (was that her real name?) is half-hidden behind Brancker. They are talking to Capt. Tepas, Dutch pilot of KLM, and behind him is Captain Spry Leverton, KLM's manager at Croydon. 41: Beneath the hat is Mrs. Dickin, shaking hands with the film star, Anna May Wong. Eve (or Eva) Gray is the name of the lady behind Mrs. Dickin's flowers; Brancker is behind Anna May Wong. To the right is Mrs. Richard, then Mrs. Spry Leverton, and far right, Major Richard.

41

40

CIVIL AVIATION ANIMAL DAY AT CROYDON AIRPORT, MAY 1929

In *Croydon Airport: The Great Days* we mentioned this rather odd publicity event, which took place on May 23rd 1929, and which involved (as the souvenir brochure/menu put it on a one-page display): a "visit of/Air Vice Marshal/Sir William Sefton Brancker . . ./to/The Croydon Aerodrome, London/for the purpose of/Receiving Messages of Goodwill from Foreign Countries/to/The People's Dispensary for Sick Animals of the Poor/on the occasion of/THE ANIMAL DAY." Miss April Day, the organiser, wrote in the brochure: "Said to myself as I watched a 'Moth' one day at Hendon circling round in almost a carressing way, 'Aeroplanes it must be.' Yes! but a big order — how to obtain aeroplanes, how to ensure their help in a charitable cause? . . ." She approached Dennis Handover of Imperial Airways, who sent her to "Major Richards [sic]"; she met Sir Sefton; Captain Spry Leverton of KLM; Commander Perrin of the Royal Aero Club; Ivor McClure of the AA Aviation Dept. All, apparently, succumbed to her charm "and agreed to help". Celebrities, and the aeroplanes with messages of goodwill, rolled-up on the day, and there was a sumptuous lunch at which the toasts included Civil Aviation, proposed by the General Secretary of the PDSA; and the PDSA, proposed by Sir Sefton Brancker. Presumably much money was raised as a result.

42

FRANCIS CHICHESTER'S FLIGHT TO AUSTRALIA, DECEMBER 1929

The *Daily Mail* headlines, on Saturday December 21st, 1929, read "Rich Young Man's Amazing Flight/12,000 Miles Dash Alone/"I'm Going to Australia"/3 a.m. Start/Across France in a Day . . . " and reported: "At three o'clock yesterday . . . Mr. Francis Chichester, a rich young New Zealander, set out from Croydon Aerodrome in an attempt to fly alone to Australia. So close a secret had he kept the whole scheme that his intention became known only a few minutes before he left. A mechanic who was helping to prepare the aeroplane jocularly asked 'Going to Australia aren't you?' and received from Mr. Chichester the unexpected answer, 'Yes'. With a 'Thanks, cheerio' to the mechanic he entered the machine and away it climbed into the brilliantly moonlit sky. He has been a pilot for only three months . . ." Chichester was, of course, the man who later became Sir Francis Chichester after winning the first solo sailing race across the Atlantic in 1960 in his yacht *Gipsy Moth III*, and sailing round the world in *Gipsy Moth IV* in 1965, at the age of 63.

In 1929, he was *flying* a Gipsy Moth (a D.H.60G), G-AAKK, *Madame Elijah,* pictured here. He was, at the time, about 28 years old, having been born in 1901 in Barnstaple, Devon, but having emigrated to New Zealand in 1919, where he made a fortune as an estate agent. He had returned to Britain in 1929 to learn to fly. His flight was successful, and he was the second man (Bert Hinkler was the first) to fly solo to Australia, arriving on 25th January 1930.

43

44

THE DUCHESS OF BEDFORD'S RETURN FROM THE CAPE, APRIL 1930

Mary, Duchess of Bedford, had been told at the age of 61 that the buzzing in her ears, a symptom of her deafness, would be helped by flying. She had never at that time been in an aeroplane. She tried it; and within three years, in August 1929, made as a passenger a record-breaking flight of 4,350 miles to Karachi in 3 days 9 hours. Her aircraft was a Fokker F.VIIa, G-EBTS, named *The Spider,* and was piloted by Charles D. Barnard with Robert F. Little as co-pilot and navigator. On the 10th of April, 1930, the same trio set off again from Lympne to fly to the Cape. By now the Duchess had herself gained a pilot's licence, and took the controls from time to time. They reached Maitland Aerodrome, Cape Town, on April the 19th, in record time, and started back on the 24th. On the way back they were forced down in Bulgaria with engine trouble but repairs were made and they reached Croydon on the 30th of April, after a round trip of 18,000 miles. The period of the flight was 21 days, the shortest time ever for the double journey; but the record for actual flying hours remained with Alan Cobham, with 175 hours against their 200 — although Cobham had taken 101 days to get there and back. *The Spider* came in to Croydon at 5.30pm, to an enthusiastic reception, which included an aircraft going up to write 'Bravo' in smoke across the sky. After landing, the Duchess; Charles Barnard; and Bob Little, were taken to the Aerodrome Hotel for an official reception by Sir Sefton Brancker.

45

The 'Flying Duchess' ended her late-flowering career, when, seven years later, at the age of seventy-two, she took off from Woburn to clock-up her two-hundreth hour of solo flying. She went out over the east coast, and was never seen again; although, later, struts of her aircraft (a D.H. Puss Moth) were washed ashore. She dreaded an inactive old age, and had recently discovered that she was too old for her pilot's licence to be renewed. The way she died is most probably the way she would have chosen — and perhaps she did.

43: The Duchess with flowers, after the landing at Croydon. Behind her right shoulder is Commander Harold Perrin, Secretary of the Royal Aero Club, and next to him is Lady Elibank. 44: *The Spider* just having landed at Croydon. 45: Charles C. Dickson's caricature of (left to right): Bob Little, Charles Barnard, and the Duchess, homeward bound from the Cape (see *Croydon Airport Remembered*, pp. 36–41)

46

FIRST REDWING AIRCRAFT 'CHRISTENED' AT CROYDON, JUNE 1930

In May 1930 Captain P.G. Robinson established a workshop on the edge of the airport, in Stafford Road. There, his resident designer, John Lane, and a consultant designer, John Kenworthy, who was employed by the Air Ministry, produced the prototype of a new light aircraft — a side-by-side, easy to fly two-seater, with folding wings. As the latter were doped red, the new aircraft was called a Redwing. The prototype was registered G-AAUO, and was ready to fly by the beginning of June; the first flight taking place on the 6th. On the 19th of June the aircraft was 'christened' by Sir Sefton Brancker (in a dark suit beyond the wing in picture 46). A christening ties up with the caricature by Charles Dickson of the Redwing baby, proudly displayed by (left to right, picture 47) John

47

Kenworthy, John Lane, Roland Darling (responsible for publicity) and Flt. Lt. Norbert Maria Sackville Russell, pilot and salesman. It was Charles Dickson who had designed the Redwing insignia (in black, red and green) which can be seen on the aircraft's side. On the 24th June, the Redwing passed its airworthiness tests at Farnborough between 9am and 3.30pm — the first aircraft to complete all its tests in one day. A second Redwing (prototype Redwing II) was built, and the firm was re-organised as Redwing Aircraft Ltd., and moved to larger premises in the old ADC sheds. Eight aircraft were built before Redwing moved away to Colchester in 1932 (they returned to Croydon in January 1934, but were concerned with repair and servicing of aircraft rather than manufacture). Redwing was bombed in the Second World War (see *Croydon Airport and the Battle for Britain*).

PRIME MINISTER RAMSAY MACDONALD, AND HIS DAUGHTER, FLY TO EDINBURGH, JANUARY 1924

James Ramsay MacDonald had become the first Labour Prime Minister in January 1924, but his minority government fell later that year. His second administration began in 1929. MacDonald was among the most air-minded of prime ministers, and made much use of Croydon. Here, he and his daughter Ishbel are leaving Croydon to fly to Edinburgh for what *The Times* described as a private visit to the Palace of Holyroodhouse as the guests of the High Commissioner. On the way they stopped at Manchester and were given a civic reception, and on the way back they were to stop at Durham and be given a civic welcome; before MacDonald addressed a meeting in his Seaham constituency.

The aircraft, apparently an Argosy, left Croydon at 10am with ten other passengers.

49

CHARLES BARNARD MAKES FIRST NON-STOP FLIGHT BETWEEN U.K. AND MALTA, AUGUST 1930

Charles Barnard, the Duchess of Bedford's pilot on her trips to India and the Cape, was, in August 1930, the first to fly non-stop from England to Malta; and the first to fly non-stop in the other direction. He left from Lympne on 31st July, 1930, in a D.H. Puss Moth, G-AAXW, and reached Malta thirteen hours later. On the following day, Friday August 1st, he flew back, landing at Croydon after fourteen and a half hours, having covered 2,800 miles at just over 100 miles per hour. The aircraft belonged to Arens Controls Ltd., and was the first aircraft to be fitted with 'Arens Safety Control' for rudder, elevator, ailerons and engine. Barnard carried to Malta letters to the Governor from Sir Sefton Brancker and J.H. Thomas (Lord Privy Seal); and here Charles Barnard, back at Croydon, is seen with his wife talking to Sir Sefton Brancker beside the Puss Moth.

AMY JOHNSON'S RETURN FROM AUSTRALIA, AUGUST 1930

Few aviation events of the 30s rivalled Amy Johnson's flight to Australia in a D.H.60G Gipsy Moth, G-AAAH, *Jason*, in May 1930, which captured the public imagination to an amazing extent. We treated the story in *Croydon Airport: The Great Days* at some length (pp.158–164). Amy left Croydon on May 5th with only a few people, including her father, to see her off. On the day she was to return, August the 4th, crowds assembled at Croydon second only to those greeting Lindbergh in 1927. Amy was due to fly-in about 6pm aboard the Imperial Airways Argosy *City of Glasgow*, G-EBLF, flown by Jimmy Youell. By 5.30 "tens of thousands" (according to *The Aeroplane*) had congregated at and around the aerodrome; and were with great difficulty prevented from blocking Purley Way completely. The Argosy, however, in which Amy had travelled from Vienna, had met strong headwinds over Europe, and was three hours late on arrival (by which time it had grown dark). On a platform, by the light of the aerodrome's floodlights, she was welcomed by Lord Thomson, Secretary of State for Air and Sir Sefton Brancker, Director of Civil Aviation (both of whom were doomed to die, in less than two months, in the crash of the airship R101). Also on the dais were Amy's parents, and Miss Margaret Bondfield, first British woman cabinet minister. Charles Grey in *The Aeroplane* (having characteristically castigated the crowds, the press and almost everything else) wrote: "The actual arrival was really rather beautiful. Heavy rain clouds with the glow of the sun seen under them to the West. A bright half-moon to the South. The lights of the Control Tower to the East. And past it came the big Argosy with her navigation lights on, and her three Jaguars roaring steadily, and three Moths in attendance . . ." Amy's own Moth, *Jason*, damaged at Brisbane, brought home in crates, had been repaired and reassembled and was standing waiting for Amy to return (picture 51). (Charles Grey said that the noise of *Jason*'s engine, which had been turned on, and the engine of the floodlight, made it impossible to hear the speeches "though one gathers [they] broadcast quite well".)

51

52: The scene along Purley Way as the crowd assembled during the day. The 'tank' is a mock-up of a World War I tank, mounted on a truck. A legend on the back reads 'All Quiet on the Western Front' (Lewis Milestone's film was released that year).

53

MISS COLUMBIA (WITH BOYD AND CONNOR) CROSSES THE ATLANTIC AGAIN, FIRST AIRCRAFT TO DO SO TWICE, OCTOBER 1930

The Bellanca W.B.2 *Miss Columbia* in which Chamberlin and Levine flew the Atlantic in 1927 made another appearance at Croydon on October the 11th, 1930, flown-in this time by Captain Erroll Boyd, with Harry Connor, formerly a lieutenant in the US navy, as navigator. The flight was planned as a non-stop one from Montreal to England, but they were forced to land at Tresco, in the Scilly Isles, after nearly 24 hours in the air, when they discovered that, owing to a fault in the fuel supply system, they would not be able to use the last 100 gallons of petrol (in their rear tank) of the 420 with which they had started. "We were counting the drops [in the forward tank]", said Captain Boyd, by the time they reached the Scillies. They jettisoned the useless tank, for safety, before their forced landing at about 3.45pm on 10th October; were re-fuelled and came on to Croydon the next day, leaving Tresco at 1.05pm and arriving at Croydon at 3.54pm. There to greet them, and, according to *The Times,* the first person to speak to them, was Charles Levine himself. The Bellanca, N-X237, left Croydon for Berlin on October 31st. *The Times* continues to refer to it as *Miss Columbia* (just *Columbia* on landing) but Kenneth McDonough's *Atlantic Wings,* 1960, says that it had been renamed *Maple Leaf.* It was the first aircraft to cross the Atlantic twice, though both times in the same direction. In the picture, Lt. Connor is on the left, Captain Boyd is in the centre, and Charles Levine is on the right.

RAMSAY MACDONALD FLIES IN (AND OUT) AT IMPERIAL CONFERENCE VISIT TO CROYDON, OCTOBER 1930

The Imperial Conference of 1930 coincided with the R101 airship disaster, in which Sir Sefton Brancker, Director of Civil Aviation, Lord Thomson, Secretary of State for Air, and Wing Commander Colmore, Director of Airship Development, were among the many killed when the airship fell to earth in bad weather and dissolved in flames near Beauvais in northern France on its maiden voyage to India on October 5th. Indeed, one of the reasons for undertaking the flight at that time was to impress the Conference (which started on October 2nd), and to further the cause of the government's airship

55

programme. Despite the gloom the disaster must have cast over air affairs at the Conference, the delegates from all over the Empire and Commonwealth assembled at Croydon on October 25th to see an air display by military machines "flown magnificently in rather difficult weather" (*The Times*).

The Prime Minister, Mr. Ramsay MacDonald, flew in to Croydon, in a open cockpit, before lunch, in a Fairey IIIF of No.24 (Communications) Squadron. These aircraft were produced in a 'communications' version of which this was one — possibly J 9061 — but were designed as light bombers. Mr. MacDonald was flown from R.A.F. Hulton, near Chequers, where he was staying.

54: Ramsay MacDonald arrives in the Fairey IIIF.

55: With the old ADC hangars in the background, and the movie cameras whirring from the top of a van, the Prime Minister leaves from the wet aerodrome in the same way that he arrived.

54

On the occasion of the first service flight to London of a new three-engined airliner, type Fokker F. XII

the K. L. M. (Royal Dutch Airlines) and
the Fokker Works, builders of the machine

request the pleasure of

Major Richard

at a demonstration which is to be given with this machine at Croydon Aerodrome, at 2.30 p.m. on Thursday, February 5th, 1931. Several flights, each with 16 passengers, will be made.

Arrangements have been made to convey our guests from London W. to Croydon and back. K. L. M. saloon-cars will leave Victoria Hotel, Northumberland Avenue, at 1.30 p.m. sharp.

Guests are requested to assemble in the conservatory of the Croydon Aerodrome Hotel at 2.30 p.m.

K.L.M. (ROYAL DUTCH AIRLINES)
N.V. NEDERLANDSCHE VLIEGTUIGENFABRIEK
(FOKKER WORKS)

Tea will be served.

FIRST VISIT, ON DEMONSTRATION FLIGHT, OF NEW KLM FOKKER, FEBRUARY 1931

The F.XII was not intended for the Amsterdam-Croydon route, but for the Amsterdam-Batavia air mail route, on which it would, as *The Aeroplane* pointed out at the time, "carry our British mails to Australia at remarkable speed" (about 120 mph). Essentially the F.XII was a three-engined improved version of the F.VIII carrying one extra passenger (16). The aircraft which arrived at Croydon on February 5th was the prototype, PH-AFL, *Leeuwerik (Lark* – KLM F.XIIs received bird names, as had F.VIIs).

PH-AFL was to leave on her maiden voyage to Batavia on March 6. She crashed four years later, in 1935. Major Richard, whose invitation card is top left, is the figure with a trilby, framed in the doorway of the F.XII.

56

57

GLEN KIDSTON SETS NEW RECORD, CROYDON-PARIS, FEBRUARY 1931

Lt. Commander Glen Kidston, formerly of the Royal Navy, owned the only British-registered Lockheed Model DL-1A Special Vega, G-ABGK (GK for Kidston's initials). This was an aircraft capable of carrying six passengers, and on February 21st, 1931, Kidston established a new record time of 80 minutes from Croydon to Le Bourget in the Vega, carrying three passengers. In 1929 Kidston had been the only survivor, jumping out before impact, when a German airliner crashed near Caterham after take-off from Croydon (six people were killed). His luck ran out, however, less than three months after his record Paris trip, when, having flown the Vega to Cape Town with a co-pilot, he was killed on May 5th flying a D.H. Puss Moth, when caught in a storm in the Drakensburg Mountains, Natal. He had set a new record of 131.8 mph average speed for 7,500 miles over 57 hours 10 minutes flying time to the Cape. The photograph shows Kidston in the cockpit of his Vega at Croydon. A Puss Moth, G-AAXZ, can be seen behind him and to the right. The Vega had been at Desoutter's works at Croydon, preparing for the South Africa trip.

58

MRS VICTOR BRUCE AT CROYDON AFTER LONGEST FLIGHT EVER MADE IN A LIGHT AEROPLANE, FEBRUARY 1931

The Hon. Mrs Victor Bruce had flown 19,000 miles around the world — across Europe and Asia to Japan and then back via North America — when she landed at Croydon on Friday 20th February, 1931. Her aircraft was a Blackburn Bluebird IV, G-ABDS *Bluebird,* and when she set out from Heston on 25th September 1930 she had had her pilot's licence for only two months and flown 40 hours solo. She covered her 19,000 miles, over 27 countries, in 47 flying days, and although she had *Bluebird* shipped across both the Pacific and the Atlantic (the Bluebird fuel range was very limited), she flew the little biplane, with a 120 hp Gipsy II engine, 600 miles across the Yellow Sea in November 1930, the first to cross it by air. Over Croydon she was accompanied by five aircraft, which had flown with her from Lympne, two of them piloted by Amy Johnson and Winifred Spooner respectively. She had received various honours in various places around the world as she went, the most curious being the Order of the Million Elephants and White Umbrella, given her in Hanoi, which entitled her to call to her aid a million elephants and ride under a white umbrella (she acquired the umbrella).

Mess.rs Auto-Auctions Ltd and the Blackburn Aeroplane Co.
request the pleasure of your company
at the Croydon Aerodrome
at 12 noon on Friday 20th February 1931 to welcome
The Honourable Mrs Victor Bruce
on the completion of her 19,000 miles solo flight
round the world in a Blackburn "Bluebird" Aeroplane.
The Honourable Mrs Victor Bruce
will be welcomed by The Under Secretary of State for Air.

THIS CARD TO BE PRODUCED AT CROYDON AERODROME.

Mildred Mary Bruce also held motor-boat and show-jumping records. She became well-known at Croydon Airport running her companies Air Dispatch Ltd. and Commercial Air Hire, formed in 1934.

58: The welcome to Mrs Bruce: far left, in a bowler hat, is Commander Perrin of the Royal Aero Club. In a trilby, behind Perrin's bowler, is J.H. Thomas, Colonial Secretary in the MacDonald government. To his right, looking more or less at camera, in another bowler, is the new Director of Civil Aviation, Lt. Col. Francis Shelmerdine; below his chin is Frederick Montague, Under-Secretary of State for Air, performing the official welcome; Major Richard is behind the poles in the centre. Mrs Bruce has the flying helmet and flowers; the Hon. *Mr*. Victor Bruce is beneath the trilby on her left.   59: Invitation card to Mrs. Bruce's reception.

60: JAPANESE, RACING AROUND THE WORLD BY PUBLIC TRANSPORT, MEET AT CROYDON, JUNE 1931.

On June 25th Mrs. Victor Bruce was photographed at Croydon with two Japanese competitors in a round-the-world race with echoes of Jules Verne's *Around the World in 80 Days* — except that they did it in less than 40. Mr. Kenzo Fukuma (left) and Mr. Suremaru Shingu (right), both employed by the *Asahi* group of newspapers left Tokyo on June 15th and Osaka on June 6th respectively in order to travel round the world in opposite directions, when possible by air, on regular passenger services, to show how quickly an 'ordinary traveller' could do just that (if he could afford it, of course). *Asahi* were air-minded — see also page 76. Mr. Fukuma and Mr. Shingu met halfway at Croydon (where else?). Here the latter is on board an Imperial Airways Argosy, bound for Paris, having reached Southampton the previous morning in the *Europa*, and London at 3.30, motoring straight to Croydon where he met Mr. Fukuma (and Mrs Bruce) and left at 5pm. Mr. Fukuma had made the flight into Croydon and was leaving the next day for Paris. He would travel via the *Aquetania* from Cherbourg. Mr. Shingu arrived back in Tokyo on Saturday 11th July, having done the eastward circuit in 35 days, 7 hours, 37 minutes. Mr. Fukuma was expected on Thursday 16th, after 31 days.

60

61

HANNIBAL, 'WORLD'S FIRST REAL AIRLINER' MAKES ITS FIRST PASSENGER FLIGHT, JUNE 1931

The Handley Page H.P.42, of which *Hannibal*, receiving its certificate of airworthiness on the 5th of June, 1931, was the prototype, is, to many people, the symbol of Croydon Airport in the 1930s. Its manufacturers called it, with some justification, 'the world's first real airliner'. Wags said that it was as steady as the Rock of Gibraltar — and just as fast. In fact, Handley Page claimed, it was for years the fastest aeroplane (cruising speed, 100 mph) for its payload in existence; and many people still say that, next to the Empire flying boats (virtually flying hotels), the H.P.42 was the most comfortable aircraft ever. Half a million passengers flew by H.P.42, and none was killed. Eight aircraft were built, four intended for eastern services (Cairo to Karachi—42Es) and four for London-Paris (42Ws). *Hannibal,* G-AAGX, despite being a 42E, was put on proving flights on the Paris route carrying the first paying passengers, on 11th June 1931.

44

FIRST VISIT OF GIANT JUNKERS G.38 TO CROYDON, JULY 1931

The Junkers G.38 monoplane was almost a huge flying-wing. Professor Hugo Junkers had visualised flying-wings, taking up to 1,000 people across the Atlantic, as far back as 1910. The nearest thing to this which Junkers built was the G.38, on which work started in 1928. With a wing-span of 144 ft. 4¼ ins. (80m.), 32 ft. 9½ ins. (2.3m.) maximum chord, and about 5 ft. 7 ins. (1.7m.) maximum thickness, this was one of the largest aircraft ever to fly in to Croydon. Within its thick wing-roots, six of its possible thirty-four passengers could be carried with an unrestricted forward view. Only two of these aircraft were built; the prototype, D-2000 (later named *Deutschland* and later still re-registered as D-AZUR) being delivered to Deutsche Luft Hansa in June 1930, but not visiting Croydon until the 1st of July 1931, from Berlin via Amsterdam. Neither this nor the second G.38, D-2500/D-APIS, *Generalfeldmarschall von Hindenburg,* which visited Croydon several times, was ever put into regular service on the Berlin-Croydon route.

The DLH pilot who brought D-2000 in to Croydon in July 1931 was the subject of one of Charles Dickson's famous Aerodrome Hotel caricatures, which showed him twirling the G.38 on one finger (picture 62). He has now been identified by Lufthansa as Flugkapitan Otto Brauer, who died in 1976 (the pilot of the second G.38, Johan Wend, killed in a flying accident in April 1933, is the subject of another caricature). D-AZUR crashed at Dessau in 1936, and D-APIS was destroyed at Athens by RAF bombing in World War II.

62

63

JIM MOLLISON FLIES IN FROM RECORD-BREAKING AUSTRALIA-ENGLAND FLIGHT, AUGUST 1931

James Allan Mollison, not yet married to Amy Johnson (who was at that time on her way out to Japan), reached Croydon on August 6th, 1931, after paring-down Charles Scott's record time from Australia to England of 10 days 13 hours and 25 minutes, set up only just over a month earlier, to 8 days, 19 hours and 25 minutes. Mollison, then aged 26, was flying a D.H.60G Gipsy Moth, Australian-registered VH-UFT (formerly G-AUFT). Mollison, who had learned to fly with the RAF at Duxford, had latterly been flying for Kingsford-Smith and Ulm's Australian National Airways. The first day of his flight back to England was described at the time as probably the longest day's flying ever made in a light aeroplane: 1,730 miles on July 29th from Wyndham, Australia to Batavia. All reports of Mollison's arrival at Croydon agree how immensely tired he was.

64

65

He was determined to reach England by 2.30pm on August 6th and beat C.W.A. Scott's time in the air for the trip. Some of the worst conditions of the trip were met between Rome and Croydon. In *The Great Days* we told of Mollison's arrival at Le Bourget, and his being helped by Imperial Airways' manager there, Charles Ifould (pp.168–170). With petrol guaranteed by Ifould, Mollison crossed the Channel and landed at Pevensey. There was thick fog, and Mollison was suffering from eye-strain, not only from tiredness but from having lost his flying-goggles over India and having flown without them, in an open cockpit, for three or four days! After a couple of hours Mollison felt able to make the final miles to Croydon. There was still thick fog, and the crowds awaiting him were surprised when he came in from the north rather than the south, having overshot and discovered his position when over Mitcham. Like Mrs Bruce six months earlier (who was there to greet him), Mollison was to be officially welcomed by Mr. Montague, Under-Secretary of State for Air. Inexpert help after he had landed, from volunteers manning his wing-tips and pushing (picture 64), caused Major Richard to be sent staggering from a blow from the tail. A kangaroo in boxing gloves was brought in for publicity purposes and apparently (a) was nearly killed by the airscrew and (b) attempted to deal Mollison a vicious left hook to the jaw (*The Aeroplane*). By now probably in that state of hyper-tiredness where only the body's adrenalin, triggered by determination, keeps one going; but retaining some dignity as the reception threatened to dissolve into farce, Jim apologised for being dirty, and received Mr. Montague's congratulations (picture 65).

66

DR. ECKENER, BUILDER OF THE *GRAF ZEPPELIN*, IN WHICH HE FLEW ROUND THE WORLD, AT CROYDON (AUGUST 1931?)

Dr. Hugo Eckener, engineer, described by Sir Peter Masefield as "the Napoleon of the Zeppelin Company and the maestro of rigid airship flying", was a friend of Count Zeppelin who became a director of his company, and then, in 1924, president of it. He built the great airship *Graf Zeppelin* and flew round the world in it in 1929; the only such airship flight ever made. On August 18th, 1931, the *Graf Zeppelin*, with Eckener, visited Britain, coming in to Hanworth, Middlesex at 7pm. Eckener was welcomed by Mr. Montague (of course), thanked for his past, and promised future, contributions to British airship design, and given a gold (or silver-gilt) inscribed commemorative cigarette box. He then took a party of VIPs, including Colonel the Master of Sempill, Chairman of the Royal Aeronautical Society; and Colonel Shelmerdine, Director of Civil Aviation, on a twenty-four hour trip to Glasgow, via Cornwall, and back. The *Graf Zeppelin* left for home after returning to Hanworth. There does not appear to have been time for Dr. Eckener to have come to Croydon on this occasion; but the photograph above appears in Major Richard's scrapbook, pasted-in with material about the Hanworth visit (a party from Croydon went across in a KLM Fokker F.XII), and is labelled: 'Dr. Eckener visits Croydon'. Left to right (in the front) are: Major Richard (with stick); the Master of Sempill (part-hidden behind him); Dr. Eckener; Capt. von Schiller; Marcel Desoutter.

NB: Information coming to hand whilst the book was in the press indicates that this was October 1930, when Eckener was at Croydon after attending the funeral of the R101 victims.

MISS PEGGY SALAMAN'S
RECEPTION COMMITTEE
(Chairman - Admiral Mark Kerr)

request the pleasure of your company
at

CROYDON AIRPORT
on

Tuesday, 1st December, 1931
at 12.30 p.m.

*To welcome home Miss Peggy Salaman who, with Mr. Gordon Store,
recently set up a new record for the flight from England to Capetown in
5 days 6 hours 40 minutes.*

Miss Salaman will arrive at Croydon by air at 12.50 p.m.

**PEGGY SALAMAN AT CROYDON AFTER BREAKING GLEN KIDSTON'S
RECORD TO THE CAPE, DECEMBER 1931**

A new record to Cape Town was set up by Peggy Salaman, a nineteen-year-old
debutante, when she flew from Lympne on the 30th of October, 1931, and reached
Cape Town on November 5th, in 64 hours flying time over 5 days, 6 hours and 40
minutes. Her aircraft, which had been a birthday present to her, was a D.H.80A Puss
Moth, G-ABEH, *Good Hope*, with a 120 hp Gipsy III engine. She was accompanied by
Gordon Store, acting as co-pilot and navigator. Store, 24 years old, was South African
born, but had been an instructor at the London Aeroplane Club in 1930 and 1931.
Peggy had had only ten hours' solo flying experience when they set out.

On December the 1st there was a reception at Croydon to welcome her home. She
arrived at Southampton on 30th November aboard the *Warwick Castle* from Cape
Town, together with the two lion cubs, Juba and Joker, which she had bought at Juba, in
the Sudan, and which then flew the last 3,500-or-so miles with her. Also with her was
Good Hope, ready to be assembled at Hamble to fly to Croydon. In describing her
flight, Peggy gave full credit to Gordon Store, whom she described as being in charge of
the flight, and who handled the aircraft in difficult situations. However, she had flown
the Puss Moth for long distances herself, over the Mediterranean and the forests of
Central Africa. In the air there was little chance to talk, she said, and she doubted
whether she said forty words to Mr. Store in the air. Communication was by signs. There
had been one forced landing near Mpika (now in Zambia). She had slept that night on
the ground with the lion cubs, while Mr. Store kept watch and studied the maps for the
rest of the route, which was flown with a slightly damaged tailplane. It was fortunate
that the 'plane could take off, since they had very little supplies with them . . .

Bertram Mills gave her three hundred guineas for the cubs, exhibiting them at Olympia
that Christmas for hospital charities before giving one to the young Princess Elizabeth.
Peggy Salaman, who became Mrs Peggy Bell, now lives in California, and is a member
of the Croydon Airport Society, as is Captain Store.

69

KINGSFORD-SMITH BRINGS FIRST DIRECT CHRISTMAS AIR MAIL FROM AUSTRALIA, DECEMBER 1931

The story of the Empire air mail in relation to Croydon is told in *Croydon Airport: The Great Days,* chapter six. In December 1931 the first Christmas air mail to be flown direct from Australia (it included also mail from New Zealand) reached Croydon. It arrived on the 16th, flown in by Charles Kingsford-Smith and G.U. 'Scotty' Allen in the Australian National Airways Avro Ten, UH-UMG, *Southern Star.* The mail had started out on board UH-UNA, *Southern Sun,* also an Avro Ten, flown by Allen, which had come to grief at Alor Star, in Malaysia, on a faulty take-off, although pilot and mail were unharmed. 'Smithy', with Bill Hewitt, flew out to Alor Star, rescued crew and mail, and flew on to Croydon in thirteen-and-a-half days. The air journey had been seventeen days in all from Melbourne, and the 40, or 50,000 letters had been on their way for twenty-four days.

The picture shows *Southern Star* at Croydon. Kingsford-Smith, in flying kit, stands in front of it, with the mail sacks being loaded into Imperial Airways carts. F.G.L. Bertram, Deputy Director of Civil Aviation, in a bowler, is to his right, next to the man with the microphone.

70

VISIT OF THE CROWN PRINCE OF ETHIOPIA, JANUARY 1932

On January 14th, 1932, another Royal inspection of Croydon was made, this time by His Highness Merid Azmatch Asfa Wossen, Crown Prince of Abyssinia (Ethiopia), the son of the Emperor Haile Selassie. The Crown Prince was in Great Britain between the 12th and the 16th of January as part of a month's official tour which had already taken him to France and was to take him on to Italy, Switzerland and Germany.

70: His Highness has something pointed out to him whilst the Director of Civil Aviation, Francis Shelmerdine, stands with hands in pockets, looking quizzical. The group is behind the terminal building at Croydon. 71: The Prince's party walks from the aerodrome side of the terminal building, with Mrs Shelmerdine looking inscrutable. 72: The Prince boards an Imperial Airways H.P.42 airliner, probably for the statutory flight over London. That night, guests at a dinner given in the Prince's honour included the Duke of Gloucester, the Archbishop of Canterbury, the Prime Minister and most of the Cabinet.

71   72

Prince Asfa remained Crown Prince for a long time. Abyssinia was, of course, attacked and occupied by Mussolini in 1936, and Haile Selassie was exiled, but restored in 1941, remaining Emperor until deposed by military insurrection in 1974. The 'Armed Forces Committee' then declared that Prince Asfa Wossen (who had had a stroke in 1972 and was living in Switzerland) should become King, and that his coronation would be held as soon as he returned to the country. The Prince, however, did no such thing, condemning the purges and executions of the military government; and in August 1975 they announced that Asfa Wossen could no longer use the title of King, and that all royal ranks were abolished. His father, three weeks later, died in captivity, after a prostate operation, at the age of eighty-three.

73

FIRST REGULAR AIRMAIL SERVICE TO THE CAPE BEGINS, JANUARY 1932

On January 20th, 1932, the H.P.42 G-AAXF, *Helena* left Croydon carrying the first air mail for the new regular service to Cape Town. The pilot was A.B.H. ('Jimmy') Youell; and Mr. Bertram, Deputy Director of Civil Aviation, and Sir Vyell Vyvyan, director of Imperial Airways, were to accompany the mail all the way. As *The Times* said: "For the first time the mail aeroplane was appropriately labelled as a mail train. A panel on the side bore the legend 'Royal Mail' over the Crown and the initials G.R. . . . " One person watching the mail leave was Lady Bailey (see. p.23). Scheduled time to Cape Town was 11 days. The mail arrived on February 2nd. *Helena* took it to Paris only, after which it went by train; Scipio flying-boat (Brindisi-Alexandria); train; Argosy aircraft (Cairo-Khartoum); Calcutta flying-boat (to Kisumu); and a D.H.66 Hercules (to Cape Town). After the mail left Croydon, VIPs were entertained to lunch at the Aerodrome Hotel by Imperial Airways; Sir George Beharrell, director (later Chairman), presiding.

MORE FILM STARS AT CROYDON: JOHN GILBERT AND VIRGINIA BRUCE, 1932

On the 27th of October, 1932, John Gilbert and his wife Virginia Bruce, both then major film stars, passed through Croydon Airport on their way to Paris and were phiotographed on the steps of an H.P.42. Gilbert had been in films since 1919. His period of major success was 1924–29, when he was dubbed 'The Great Lover'. The coming of the talkies was disastrous to him: his prim voice and his acting style would not adapt successfully; his popularity dropped, and he quarrelled with his studio, MGM. He made three more films after 1932, however, including *Queen Christina* with Garbo in 1933. After he had drunk himself to death (he died in 1936), Marlene Dietrich bought his bedsheets at auction. As well as Virginia Bruce, he had been married to three other actresses.

Virginia Bruce, in 1932, unlike her husband, still had fifty years to live, and the major part of her career to come. Born Helen Virginia Briggs, she had been a Ziegfeld Follies girl before entering films in 1929. In the 30s and 40s she made dozens of films, including *The Great Ziegfeld, Jane Eyre* (in which she played the title role) and *The Night has a Thousand Eyes*. Her last film was *Strangers when we Meet*, in 1960. She died in 1982, aged 71. She, too, married four times; John Gilbert, to whom she was married from 1932 to 1934, being her first husband.

74

TWO ROYAL BROTHERS LEAVE FOR COPENHAGEN VIA CROYDON, SEPTEMBER 1932

75: Prince Edward, Prince of Wales, was at Croydon Airport on the 22nd of September on his way to open an Anglo-Danish Trade Exhibition in Copenhagen. He flew in from Fort Belvedere on board a Spartan Cruiser and left on the H.P.42 *Heracles*, G-AAXC, with Jimmy Youell as pilot. (It had been intended to fly the Prince to Denmark in the new Imperial Airways four-engined monoplane, the Armstrong Whitworth Atalanta — presumably the prototype G-ABPI — but wireless equipment problems caused this to be cancelled.) The Prince flew via Amsterdam and Hamburg, and had a 'rough and unpleasant crossing'. Twenty Danish aircraft escorted *Heracles* into Kastrup Aerodrome, after a circular flight over Copenhagen, where Edward was welcomed by the Crown Prince of Denmark and other members of the royal family.

76: On the 30th of September, H.R.H. Prince George (later Duke of Kent), fourth son of George V, also passed through Croydon on his way to Copenhagen. He was travelling as an ordinary passenger on a KLM airliner via the KLM/ABA (Swedish airline) 'Scandindavia Air Express': 'the fastest and most direct link between England and Scandinavia'. From Copenhagen he was to go on to meet his brother, the Prince of Wales' at Malmö, Sweden, and together they would travel on by train to Stockholm to visit King Gustav of Sweden. The journey to Copenhagen, via Rotterdam and Amsterdam, took 6 hours, 16 minutes; and the whole journey was made in 7 hours, 7 minutes — eight minutes under schedule.

AMY'S RETURN FROM THE CAPE, DECEMBER 1932

Amy Johnson, married to Jim Mollison since the 29th of July, set out on the 14th of November, 1932, to 'beat Jim's Cape record — just as a sporting effort' as she said (he had got to Cape Town in 4 days, 17 hours and 30 minutes in March). She left from Lympne, in a D.H.80A Puss Moth, G-ACAB, *Desert Cloud*, and reached Cape Town in 4 days, 6 hours and 54 minutes. Having broken the record in one direction she set out (waiting for the full moon on December 11th for better night-flying conditions) to break it in the other; and although bad weather on the way extended her time back to 7 days, 7 hours and 5 minutes, she still had made another new record, beating the time set by the Duchess of Bedford and Charles Barnard, of 10 days, in April 1930.(*Over*)

77: On a dais, watching Amy come in, are her parents and mother-in-law. Her father (Will) is filming her arrival with a camera presented to him by Amy as a memento after her Australia flight. (The 16mm films taken on this occasion were later given to the National Film Archive by her sister, Molly Jones). In the centre is her mother (Ciss); on the left is Mrs. Bullmore, Jim Mollison's mother (she had remarried).

77

Amy's welcome-back at Croydon was another return to cheering crowds, despite the cold weather, and to another set of speeches, this time by daylight, on the temporary dais. She was officially welcomed by Francis Bertram, Deputy Director of Civil Aviation; and Geoffrey de Havilland, Malcolm Campbell, and the Countess of Drogheda were among those present.

78

78: Jim Mollison (left) awaits Amy's arrival with Sir Malcolm Campbell, holder of world speed records in motor and speed-boat racing; and (79) greets his wife beneath the wings of her aircraft. "On her arrival Mrs. Mollison showed very little signs of fatigue", said *The Times'* reporter. "She told me that on her long non-stop journeys she had warded off sleepiness by taking plenty of strong coffee and a caffeine tablet every six hours."

80: The workmen erecting the dais before Amy's arrival.

80

81: Amy on the flag-bedecked dais (with Jim looking as though he is being enveloped by the flag).

81

82

FIRST ANNUAL CROYDON AIRPORT STAFF DINNER, FEBRUARY 1933

The Aeroplane on March 8th, 1933, said: "On Feb. 27 some 400 people attended the first annual function of the Croydon Air Port Staff at the Greyhound Hotel Theatre, Croydon. The chair was taken by Major L.F. Richard, Chief Aerodrome Officer. The attendance and success of the evening showed that the feeling in favour of an occasional social meeting of the aerodrome folk had been accurately gauged by the Committee. The instigators were Messrs. F. Blunden, E. Geary, Charles Allen and A. Langridge, and they deserve every congratulation. The speeches were commendably short."

The Chairman proposed the King; Capt. Bill Lawford the Silent Toast; Capt. Walter Rogers the Ladies — to which Mrs. Richard replied. Capt. Chattaway proposed the Operating Companies; and a toast to the Visitors was replied to by Captain Stanley Baker, who had been C.A.T.O. at Croydon before Major Richard, and proceeded to tell stories of those present to prove he was no stranger. Captain Spry Leverton of KLM proposed the health of Major Richard and praised the smoothness of his organisation. Major Richard welcomed everyone and praised his predecessor, Captain Baker. A concert and dance followed, "with great success". The tickets on the right relate to later activities of the Croydon Airport Social Committee, and the menu cover to the second Annual Dinner (83).

83

84

START OF ENGLAND-AUSTRALIA SURVEY FLIGHT, MAY 1933

Another flight to further the development of the Empire air routes began on May 29th, 1933, this time to survey a passenger route to Australia. The aircraft was the Armstrong Whitworth A.W.15 Atalanta, G-ABTL, *Astraea,* fifth of her class to be delivered, which had received a certificate of airworthiness on the 4th of April. The Atalantas were built for the Empire routes. *Astraea* flew to Paris, Lyons, Rome, Brindisi, Athens, Alexandria; then the Cairo-Karachi route; then Jodhpur, Delhi, Calcutta, Akyab, Rangoon, Bangkok, Prachuab, Alor Star, Singapore, Palembang, Batavia, Sourabaya, Bima, Koepang, Bathurst Island, Darwin, Newcastle Waters, Camooweal, Cloncurry, Longreach, Roma, Toowoomba, Brisbane, Sydney, Canberra and Melbourne, which it reached on June 29th. On her way back, *Astraea* operated a scheduled Calcutta-Karachi service, after 23,430 miles in the air in a flying-time of 210 hours, 37 minutes.

In the picture, left to right, before the start of the flight are: Mr. Griffiths, Flight Engineer; Major H.G. Brackley ('Brackles'), Air Superintendent of Imperial Airways, in charge of the flight; the Marconi representative at Croydon; Capt. J.V. Prendergast, pilot; Mr. W.E. Hickman, Armstrong Whitworth representative. The signature of the latter is across the top of the photograph, which was given by him to the late Jack Crowson, of Imperial Airways (and later BOAC), who lodged in the same house as he in Link Lane, Wallington.

JIM MOLLISON FAILS TO GET *SEAFARER* OFF THE GROUND ON ATTEMPT AT ATLANTIC FLIGHT, JUNE 1933

On June 5th, 1933, Jim Mollison crashed the de Havilland D.H.84 Dragon, *Seafarer*, G-ACCV, in which he and his wife Amy (Johnson) were attempting the first leg — Croydon to New York — of a projected flight to beat the world's long-distance record by flying non-stop from New York to Baghdad. A previous intended start, on Whit Monday, June 5th, was cancelled because of the weather. A combination of the over-loading of the aircraft with 400 gallons of petrol, a dip in the ground over which the long take-off run took them, and the fact that Jim, not the most abstemious of men, had been celebrating the night before, caused an undercarriage collapse which did considerable damage to the lower parts of the aircraft. In the picture, Jim, with folded arms, looks disconsolate by the crumpled wing. Amy, in white overalls on the right, contemplates the damage.

When, some six weeks later, their aircraft repaired, they took off from Pendine Sands, South Wales, they made it into the air and across the Atlantic, but crash-landed at Bridgeport, Conn., and the Dragon this time was a write-off. Thus ended the Mollisons' attempt to complete this flight.

86

FIRST AUSTRALIA—ENGLAND FLIGHT BY WOMAN (MRS. BONNEY) FINISHES AT CROYDON, JUNE 1933

Violet Bonney (or Mrs. Harry B. Bonney, as she tended to be called at the time, having become the first woman to fly round Australia, left Darwin on the 15th April, 1933, in a D.H. 60G Gipsy Moth, VH-UPV (doing an 'Amy Johnson' in reverse). This particular Gipsy Moth, as G-ABEN, had been flown out to Australia at a leisurely pace in October-December 1930. Mrs. Bonney arrived at Croydon on the 21st June. There were very few people to meet her. *The Aeroplane,* having grumbled about the disruption of busy airline routines at Croydon by such events as the Mollisons' abortive attempts to take-off for America now regretted, on behalf of British aviation, that she had not been properly received. It appeared, however, that she had let few people in this country 'except the airport officials at Croydon' know of her impending arrival; and Harold Perrin, of the Royal Aero Club, had spent several days trying to find out whom she was staying with in London because he had a mass of mail awaiting her at the Club. A representative of Wakefield's Oil had tried to keep track of Mrs. Bonney's progress in the final stages of her flight, and had dashed between Heston and Croydon, being unsure at which she intended to arrive. He, apparently, and a couple of photographers, were just about all the crowd which greeted her. Apart from her reticence, however, both Press and public were beginning to get just a little blasé about long-distance flights, although these were hardly less hazardous now than they had been five or six years earlier. The photograph shows Violet Bonney flying her Gipsy Moth.

PRINCESS INGRID OF SWEDEN ARRIVES AT CROYDON, JULY 1933

In 1932 and 1933, Princess Ingrid, daughter of the Crown Prince of Sweden, made several appearances at Croydon Airport. In October 1932 she came on the Imperial Airways Argosy G-AACJ, *City of Manchester,* travelling incognito from Brussels. She was on her way to see her grandfather, the Duke of Connaught, third son of Queen Victoria. His daughter, Princess Margaret of Connaught, had married Crown Prince Gustav Adolf in 1905. Gustav Adolf became King Gustav VI Adolf of Sweden in 1950 and died, aged 90, in 1973. On July 3rd 1933 Princess Ingrid again arrived at Croydon to stay with her grandfather at Clarence House, this time accompanied by her brother, Prince Carl-Johan. On the 12th, they, their parents and the Duke of Connaught, had lunch with King George V and Queen Mary. Princess Ingrid left for home on August 12th. She is now Dowager Queen Ingrid of Denmark, having been married to King Frederick of Denmark who died in 1972.

In the picture, a splendid study in early 1930s fashion, Princess Ingrid is on the extreme right of the picture. The aircraft whose tail is behind them is possibly a Fokker F.VIII of KLM.

88

FIRST (AND ONLY) VISIT OF DEWOITINNE D.332 TO CROYDON, SEPTEMBER 1933

In 1933 the Société Aéronautique Française, formerly Constructions Aéronautiques E. Dewoitinne, built a new three-engined low-wing cantilever monoplane for the newly-formed Air France.

The Dewoitinne D.332 prototype, F-AMMY *Émeraude* (*Emerald*) was delivered in September. It had three French-built Wright Cyclone radial engines and was of all-metal construction, with accommodation for a crew of three, and eight passengers. It was designed for the Toulouse-Dakar section of the South American route, and had up-to-date heating and ventilation, and reclining passenger-seats for night flying.

Émeraude visited Croydon during September; returned to Paris, and flew to Malmö in four-and-a-half hours; from Paris to Algiers in six hours; and Paris to Dakar in

89

twenty-five hours. It then set out, on December 22nd, for Saigon, which was reached on December 28th after 40 hours' flying time. On the return flight, however, *Emeraude* crashed in the Morvan mountains, in Central France, and all ten people on board were killed. They included the French director of commercial aviation, and the Governor-General of French Indo-China. The disaster happened in a heavy snowstorm, but the aircraft was seen to fall in flames. No more D.332s were built, but three D.333s, similar, but with a greater wing area and other differences, were put into production, followed by the D.338, carrying 22 passengers on European services, and with a retractable undercarriage. These do not appear to have been used on regular services to Croydon, however.

88: The D.332 at Croydon with the Aerodrome Hotel behind its tail and the control tower in front of its nose. 89: The D.332 with 'C' hangar block beyond its port wing.

90

PRINCE GEORGE RETURNS FROM WOOING PRINCESS MARINA OF GREECE, SEPTEMBER 1934

On August 16th, 1934, *The Times* announced that Prince George had left Croydon Airport for Paris on the ordinary passenger service. By August 16th he had reached Llubljana "in the Prince of Wales's aeroplane from Le Bourget . . . in order to visit the Yugoslav Royal family at Bled". On August 27th he was reported as having arrived at Salzburg with Prince Paul of Yugoslavia. On August 30th it was revealed that he had become engaged to Princess Marina of Greece, who was the sister of Prince Paul's wife, Princess Olga. "Messages of congratulation poured in . . . from all parts of the world to the King and Queen at Balmoral . . . and to Prince George at Salzburg . . ." By this time all four (George, Marina, Paul and Olga) had left Salzburg and returned to Bled. There, even in 1934, "The betrothed couple could hardly have wished for pleasanter surroundings, but their peace is already threatened by inquisitive holidaymakers and journalists" (said *The Times*).

91

By September 11th George was on his way back, and was photographed with Marina in Paris. "The Prince", it was said, "is continuing his journey to London today, and the Princess is expected to visit the King and Queen shortly". On the 12th, Prince George returned to Croydon on board *Hengist* (picture 90). He was met by Charles Wolley Dod, now the European area manager of Imperial Airways (picture 91) and Major Richard (left). Within a few hours of his return he had ordered a square Kashmir sapphire engagement ring.

Prince George (4th son of King George V and Queen Mary) was created Duke of Kent when he married Princess Marina. He was killed on active service in 1942 on board a Sunderland flying boat which crashed. Princess Marina died in 1968.

92

93

PRESENTATION OF FIRST OFFICIAL ROYAL AIR MAIL PENNANT TO IMPERIAL AIRWAYS, MAY 1934

At a ceremony on Saturday May 26th, 1934, the first pennant, designed to be flown "by all mail aeroplanes as well as the civil aviation ensign", and "over buildings from which air mails are embarked or disembarked", was presented by Sir Kingsley Wood (Postmaster General) to Sir Eric Geddes, Chairman of Imperial Airways, who passed it on to Captain A.J. Horsey (picture 92), by whom it was "immediately set above the nose of *Hengist . . .* before the departure of the liner with the mails" (93). *Hengist* was going to Paris, and the mail was going on to India. The pennants were fine, but the pilots needed to remember to lower them before take-off (they were supposed to fly during taxi-ing and immediately on landing). The pilots did not always remember, which could be disastrous — at least to the pennants. Directors of Imperial Airways present during the ceremony were Sir John Salmond, Sir Walter Nicholson, Mr. G.F. Woods Humphery, Sir George Beharrell and Sir Samuel Instone. Others present included the High Commissioner for India; the Mayor of Croydon (J. Trumble); Mr. Bertram, the D.D.C.A.; Major Brackley; Mr. Wolley Dod; and, of course, Major Richard. A silver replica of *Hengist* was presented to Lady Wood as a souvenir.

NEW HIGH-SPEED GERMAN AIRCRAFT AT CROYDON, JUNE 1934

The Heinkel He.70 was the result of a specification from Deutsche Luft Hansa for a high-speed four-passenger aircraft with retractable undercarriage and a speed capability of 300 km/hr (186.4 mph). The prototype flew in December 1932. The second aircraft built was given, perhaps ominously, the name *Blitz* (*Lightning*); and this became the unofficial designation for the aircraft type (the rest of the civil production aircraft were given bird names). In the Spring of 1933 the He.70 set eight new speed records, reaching a maximum speed of 234.2 mph. The first He.70 to visit Croydon was the fifth built, D-UDAS, *Habicht* (*Hawk*), seen here both in the air and on the ground, with 'B' hangar block on the left. It was on Sunday June 17th that *Habicht* flew from Paris to Croydon in 70 minutes, and on Monday 18th July was, as Major Turner,

94

95

the *Daily Telegraph*'s aviation correspondent wrote, "put through its paces . . . in the presence of a crowd of experts". They were highly impressed, not only by its speed, but by its manoeuvrability and rate of climb; but Major Turner felt that the He.70 was uneconomic as a civil aircraft and was really to be regarded as the prototype of a high-speed bomber, a sentiment echoed in *The Times*' report. *Habicht* was flown to Croydon by Herr R. Untucht. He.70s had already begun service on the Berlin-Cologne and part of the Berlin-South America routes.

96

When he left to fly back home, first stop Paris, on board an H.P.42 (seen off by Sir Eric Geddes?) on a date I have not found, the weather was evidently quite different (97, right).

General Smuts became South African prime minister again on the outbreak of the Second World War, at the end of which he helped to create the United Nations. He was made Field-Marshal in 1941. He died in 1950.

GENERAL SMUTS ARRIVES AT CROYDON IN THE RAIN — AND LEAVES IN THE SUN, OCTOBER 1934

Jan Christiaan Smuts, South African statesman, was born in Cape Colony and educated at Cambridge. Having fought against the British in the Boer War, he later regained his British sympathies. During World War I he was entrusted with operations in German East Africa and made a member of the Imperial War Cabinet. In 1919 he became prime minister of the Union of South Africa. With Herzog he formed the United South African National Party (the United Party) in 1934.

On October 4th, 1934, he arrived at Croydon Airport, having left Johannesburg on September 26th. He was due to be installed as Rector of St Andrews University on October 17th. His arrival was in the rain (96).

97

98

FIRST FLIGHT ON RAILWAY AIR SERVICES' CROYDON-GLASGOW *ROYAL MAIL* ROUTE AUGUST 1934

In *Croydon Airport: The Great Days* we printed a photograph of the inauguration ceremony of Railway Air Services' *Royal Mail* service to Glasgow via Birmingham, Manchester and Belfast. This is another picture taken on the same occasion. Railway Air Services was owned jointly by Imperial Airways and the four British mainline railway companies. The first Railway Air Services route was flown in May 1934, from Croydon to the Isle of Wight. The London-Glasgow airmail route, in conjunction with Spartan Air Lines, was to be one of three new inland mail-flying Railway Air Services routes, the others being Liverpool-Plymouth and Birmingham-Cowes. A service by Highland Airways was already flying from Inverness to the Orkneys. There were problems with the weather (severe gales) on the first scheduled day of the Glasgow route and the mail did not get to its intended destination by air in either direction (from Croydon, Birmingham was reached), full working starting on the next day. The aircraft leaving Croydon was a Westland Wessex, piloted by Captain William Armstrong. The mail was handed to him by Brigadier-General Sir Frederick Williamson, Director of Postal Services (in the light trilby). Also on the platform is Francis Bertram, Deputy Director of Civil Aviation (right, with bowler hat).

FIRST REGULAR WEEKLY AIRMAIL SERVICE TO AUSTRALIA BEGINS, DECEMBER 1934

On 8th December 1934 *Hengist*, G-AAXE, flew the mail travelling on the first regular weekly service to Australia out of Croydon. The pilot was Captain Leslie Walters; and *Hengist*, making a positioning flight, was going as far as Karachi. Before the airmail left, a ceremony, broadcast by the BBC, was held in one of the 'A' block hangars. Lord Londonderry, Secretary of State for Air, and Sir Kingsley Wood, Postmaster General, officially opened the route. Sir Eric Geddes, Chairman of Imperial Airways, officially received the mail, which included letters from the King and Queen, the Prince of Wales, and the Prime Minister (Ramsay MacDonald). After Karachi the mail went on in G-ABTL, *Astraea*, the Armstrong Whitworth A.W.15 Atalanta in which the route had been surveyed in 1933 (see p. 59) and VH-AEF, *Arethusa*, which originally had been the Atalanta prototype *Atalanta*, G-ABPI (rebuilt after an early accident when, apparently to avoid bad publicity for a new aircraft type, the name *Atalanta* was transferred to G-ABTI, the fourth A.W.15). The mail reached Darwin on the 16th of December.

Left (99) *Hengist* is towed out on to the tarmac from the hangar. Above (100) *Hengist* poses in front of the control tower.

101

KINGSFORD-SMITH'S LAST VISIT TO CROYDON, OCTOBER 1935

In 1935 Charles Kingsford-Smith had reached the age of 38, and felt he must accomplish at least one more record-breaking feat before he was 40. He decided to try to beat the England to Australia record set up by C.W.A. Scott and T. Campbell Black in G-ACSS, *Grosvenor House,* the D.H.88 Comet racer in which they won the 'MacRobertson' London (Mildenhall) to Melbourne race in 1934, in 70 hours 54 minutes flying time over 2 days, 4 hours, 33 minutes. His attempt was made in his Lockheed 8D Altair, *Lady Southern Cross,* VH-USB, now re-registered in Britain as G-ADUS. With him was John Pethybridge as co-pilot. On 20th October, 1935, they took-off from Croydon, but had to come back to Croydon for repairs after damage due to wing-icing at Brindisi. On 6th November *Lady Southern Cross* left again for Melbourne, this time from Lympne. They reached Allahabad in 29 hours, 28 minutes; but after take-off for Singapore on 8th November, Smithy, Pethybridge and *Lady Southern Cross* were never seen again — except that, two years later, part of the aircraft's undercarriage was washed ashore on an island near Burma, and identified.

The photograph shows *Lady Southern Cross* outside Rollason's in 'C' hangar block at Croydon, perhaps after the return from Brindisi for repairs.

MERRILL AND RICHMAN AT CROYDON AFTER CROSSING THE ATLANTIC IN *LADY PEACE*, SEPTEMBER 1936

Among the last pioneering transatlantic flights, heralding the beginning of commercial 'proving flights' foreshadowing regular services, in 1937, was that of Dick Merrill and Harry Richman, which started on the afternoon of Wednesday September 2nd, 1936, from Floyd Bennett Field, New York. Harry Richman was a night club owner, and apparently well-known in America as a singer and entertainer. Dick Merrill was an airline pilot of considerable experience. Their aircraft, a silver and blue Vultee V-1a monoplane with a single Wright (what else?) engine — this time a Cyclone, delivering 1000 hp — the most powerful single-engined aircraft yet to make the crossing was significantly an aeroplane of a type which had been in regular service with US airlines for two years, and had accommodation for eight passengers. This one was named *Lady Peace*. It was publicised at the time that the wings held thousands of table-tennis balls for buoyancy if a descent in the sea was made. Richman and Merrill hoped to cross in 14 hours, reach Croydon, and return in 16 hours. In fact, it took eighteen (the time 'between supper and tea' as a *Times* leader put it), and they landed first at Llandilo, in South Wales, after losing their way in bad weather, and having their wireless disabled by lightning. "Somehow we missed Ireland", Richman said, "just didn't see it, and that threw us off . . . We were circling for about an hour and a half and that used up the gas . . . in the end we picked a field [to land in] where there were three cows . . ." Two aircraft set out from Croydon to take them petrol, and they flew on next day (the 4th) to Croydon, stopping at Bristol for lunch. *Lady Peace* had been robbed overnight of her lamps and wing-lights by souvenir hunters. They received a good welcome at Croydon (although it was raining), and a friend, a Mr. James Town, went up from Croydon in another Vultee to escort them in. They left England from Birkenhead Sands on September 13th, and made the return crossing in 17 hours 45 minutes, force-landing in a Newfoundland bay.

102: *Lady Peace* comes in over 'C' hangars, the old ADC sheds. 103: Dick Merrill and Harry Richman acknowledge the Croydon crowd's welcome.

104

FIRST JAPANESE AIRCRAFT TO REACH BRITAIN, APRIL 1937

The Mitsubishi Karigane (Wild Goose) all-metal low-wing monoplane *Kamikaze* (*Divine Wind*) flew in to Croydon Airport at 3.30pm on Friday April 9th, 1937. On board was the pilot, Masaki Iinuma, and the engineer/radio operator, Kenji Tsukagoshi. Together they had flown from Tokyo (leaving on April 5th at 5.12pm), a distance of 10,000 miles, in 94 hours 10 minutes (actual flying time about 50 hours), bearing a goodwill message to the British nation from the president of the *Asahi Shimbun* newspaper which read in part, ". . . the *Asahi Shimbun* sends you two of its most noted aviators instructed with the triple object of carrying Japan's greetings to the British nation on the happy occasion of the Coronation of King George VI, presenting messages of good will to the nations of Europe, and establishing, it is hoped, a new aerial record between Tokyo and London . . ." (In fact, any flights, so far, had been in the other direction.) The arrival brought crowds to Croydon in something like their old force; and by the time the Japanese had reached Le Bourget (at 1.35pm) there were already 2,000 people, including about 250 Japanese (probably most of London's small Japanese colony) waiting at Croydon. *The Times* said: ". . . the spectators surged forward, sweeping the police and aerodrome officials with them, until there was a real danger that some one would be struck by the still revolving airscrew, that the flower-bearing children would be crushed, and that the controlling surfaces of the *Divine Wind* would be damaged . . .

The airmen were escorted (and at times carried) to the Aerodrome Hotel (seen in picture 104 with spectators crowding the roof). There was much interest expressed in the aviation press about the aircraft, which *Flight* said was reminiscent of the American Northrop series, but admitted this was only superficial. The radial engine, a 550 hp Nakajima Kotobuki, was said to seem to be "a Japanese-built Wright Cyclone". All of this, of course, was long before Japan was associated with high-technology.

In picture 105 Iinuma is on the left, Tsukagoshi, whose un-Japanese appearance was commented on at the time, is on the right.

105

On April 16 the *Kamikaze* went on to Brussels, where the airmen were received by King Leopold, and to Germany where they were received by Goering and the Lord Mayor of Berlin (Germany and Japan had signed an 'anti-Bolshevist' pact the previous November). The relatively low level of hospitality offered them in London, in contrast, was the subject of some adverse comment in *The Aeroplane,* a fact, it said, of which British aviation should be heartily ashamed.

CLOUSTON AND RICKETTS AND G-ACSS: NEW ZEALAND AND BACK IN THREE DAYS, WITH AT LEAST NINE RECORDS BROKEN, MARCH 1938

The D.H.88 Comet, G-ACSS, which won the 'MacRobertson' London-Melbourne race in 1934, had almost as many names as the number of record-breaking trips she made. *Grosvenor House, The Orphan, The Burberry*; and now, as *Australian Anniversary* she set out on her last great flight on March 15th, 1938, (after a previous abortive start), from Gravesend, piloted by Flying Officer (later Air Commodore) A.E. Clouston, with Victor Ricketts, air correspondent of *The Daily Express* as passenger and relief pilot (he had a let-down typewriter above his dual controls). The flight was sponsored by the Australia Consolidated Press and it was the 150th anniversary of the foundation of the first British (penal) settlement in Australia, at Botany Bay. The re-christening ceremony took place at Croydon, with a bottle of champagne broken against the aircraft's nose. The purpose was a record-breaking round trip to Australia, but Clouston, a New Zealander, wanted to visit home, and made up his mind to include New Zealand on the flight. He hoped to beat Scott's record to Darwin in G-ACSS. He failed; but they reached Sydney in the record time of 80 hours 56 minutes from England. Telling only the sponsoring newspaper, they flew on to New Zealand. Crossing the Tasman Sea, they arrived at Blenheim where they were to land. As they circled the town of 10,000 people they were amazed to find nobody visible and no sign of life in the streets. When they got to the airport they found everybody there — the newspaper had kept its promise to inform Clouston's parents of his arrival and this was the result. They stopped overnight only, however, and flew back to England — to Croydon, reaching there at 5.40 pm on Saturday 26th March. The airport was packed with hundreds of people who had turned out to meet them, despite a fog which made it difficult to know, from the cockpit of G-ACSS, where the Airport was, until Clouston saw a Rapide going down, and followed him, and found housetops and a few yards visibility. They had been to New Zealand via Australia and back in 5 days, 17 hours and 30 minutes flying time over 10 days 21 hours; breaking many records: first aircraft to New Zealand and back; England-Sydney; England-New Zealand; Darwin-Sydney; Australia-New Zealand; New Zealand-London; Sydney-London; and the round trip from London to Sydney. When they saw hangars through the fog, and Clouston found his way in, they met a tumultuous welcome on the ground. As the flashbulbs exploded it was quite like old times at Croydon.

106

Fittingly, G-ACSS is now preserved, restored as *Grosvenor House*, in the Shuttleworth Collection at Old Warden Aerodrome, Beds. She was one of the greatest aircraft of a great era, and her pilots, especially Scott, Campbell Black and Clouston were among the greatest figures. The photograph shows Clouston and Ricketts leaving the cockpit of G-ACSS at Sydney after breaking the first record on the flight, and bears Air Commodore Clouston's signature.